ODDS
ON

ODDS
ON

*the making of an
evidence-based investor*

MATT HALL

GREENLEAF
BOOK GROUP PRESS

This publication is designed to provide accurate and authoritative information in regard to the subject matter covered. It is sold with the understanding that the publisher and author are not engaged in rendering legal, accounting, or other professional services. If legal advice or other expert assistance is required, the services of a competent professional should be sought.

Published by Greenleaf Book Group Press
Austin, Texas
www.gbgpress.com

Distributed by Greenleaf Book Group

For ordering information or special discounts for bulk purchases, please contact Greenleaf Book Group at PO Box 91869, Austin, TX 78709, 512.891.6100.

Design and composition by Greenleaf Book Group
Cover design by Greenleaf Book Group
Cover images: ©shutterstock/Maridav

Cataloging-in-Publication data is available.

Print ISBN: 978-1-62634-256-9

eBook ISBN: 978-1-62634-257-6

Part of the Tree Neutral® program, which offsets the number of trees consumed in the production and printing of this book by taking proactive steps, such as planting trees in direct proportion to the number of trees used: www.treeneutral.com

TreeNeutral®

Printed in the United States of America on acid-free paper

16 17 18 19 20 21   10 9 8 7 6 5 4 3 2 1

First Edition

For Mom, Lisa, and Harper.
Thanks for investing in the story of my life.
I am grateful every day.

Contents

ACKNOWLEDGMENTS

Thanks to my wife Lisa for setting up the lunch that allowed everything else to happen. Your and Harper's love, support, and encouragement is the fuel I need to keep creating a truly exceptional life.

Thanks to Rick Hill for being an incredible friend and business partner. Knowing you has made me better. I hope our partnership never ends.

To Buddy, Jeff, John, Henry, and Katie, thanks for tolerating my incessant talk of the book and for your valuable feedback throughout this journey. Your patience and applause helped me throughout the process.

Thanks to Clint Willis and Sean Donahue. Working with the two of you on this project has been one of the highlights of my career. You do what I think great editors do – take good content and allow it to be great.

To my mom, dad, Sam, and Annie, I don't know how people do

things without unconditional love and support from their family and I hope I never find out.

To Dr. Tomasson and Dr. Yang, I want you to know that I aspire to have clients feel the way you made me feel—well held. I am healthy and forever grateful.

Thanks to Adam Birenbaum for the push to make the book happen.

To Ed Goldberg, Mont Levy, Stuart Zimmerman, and Larry Swedroe, I will always be thankful to you for letting me in.

Thanks to my friend Carl Richards for inspiration and encouragement along the way. If I end up on the other side of complexity it has a lot to do with you.

To my college English professor, Dr. Bernard-Donals, who thought my micro-theme was so good that it couldn't have been done by me. I love thinking about that backward compliment.

To my Entrepreneur's Organization forum mates, I thank you for making me unafraid to chase things beyond my old boundaries.

I am indebted to the great and powerful Marilyn Wechter. You have made a huge impact on me, the team, and how we serve our clients.

To the team at Greenleaf Book Group, who took me on and nurtured the book to the highest level. Thank you for believing in my story and the impact it will have on readers.

To my late grandfather, Herman Hall, I know you knew I could do it. You always seemed to know I could before I did.

INTRODUCTION

I want this book to change your life.

That's an ambitious goal for any book, let alone one about investing, but I know that books have the power to change lives. It happened to me in 1999.

At the time, I had just walked away from a potential career with a Wall Street brokerage firm because I was disgusted by what I'd experienced: a broken system designed to make as much money as possible for the firm at the expense of the clients it was supposed to serve. I feared I might never achieve my dream of finding a way to help people while working in the financial world.

Then a chance encounter in the epicenter of odds-making—Las Vegas—put a new, relatively obscure book in my hands. This book showed me that there was a smarter way to invest—one that not only delivered better returns but also actually put the investor's interests first. I was so inspired by what I read that I became part of a movement to change the investing world. I've spent the past sixteen years helping clients adopt this better investment approach. And I've put everything I've learned about investing into this book, so I can reach even more people.

Some investment books provide so much technical information that they leave readers feeling overwhelmed and powerless. That's the last thing I want to do, which is why I decided not to write a typical investment book. I'm not going to tell you how to pick stocks or spot the best mutual fund managers. And I'm not going to provide a formula for outsmarting the financial markets. Instead, I'm going to tell you a story—*my* story. I hope that the lessons that have shaped my life and investment approach can help reshape yours.

You'll learn, as I did, why the conventional Wall Street investment approach is so ineffective: It's really just another form of gambling. Most investors try to pick the right investments and time the market's moves, but their chances of winning are as slim as their chance of beating the house when they walk into a casino. The deck is stacked against them.

You'll also learn, as I did, about a better investment approach that puts the long-term investment odds back in your favor. My colleagues and I call it evidence-based investing. Evidence-based investing starts by examining decades of data about how the financial markets *really* work in order to make investment decisions. Based on this scientific evidence, we choose to invest in broad swaths of the global economy that tend to generate higher expected returns over the long term.

If you know what an index fund is, then you already know something about how this approach works. Index funds capture the returns of a group of stocks that share characteristics, such as the size of the companies. These funds *don't* try to pick which companies within that group will do better than others, yet they still tend to outperform funds that have managers and analysts cobbling together customized stock portfolios over longer periods of time. Building on this foundation, the evidence-based movement has been studying market data and academic research to identify the groups of stocks and other investments that provide better odds of long-term success. If you come to believe what I believe, you're unlikely to gamble with your life savings again.

The science behind evidence-based investing is only part of the *Odds On* story. When I was thirty-three and in the midst of developing my skills as an evidence-based investor, I was diagnosed with a potentially fatal illness. I thought I might die without achieving many of my life's most important goals. But the doctors who took care of me taught me an important lesson about how to truly help people facing intense anxiety and uncertainty. That experience helped me combine an evidence-based strategy with an approach to client care and guidance that helps people stick with their investment plan and let the odds work in their favor.

When I started my real career in 1999, evidence-based investing was a tiny niche with only a few followers on Wall Street, let alone Main Street. Since then, it's grown into a force that is threatening to transform investing. The savviest investors understand the data and evidence, and they are investing their money accordingly.

Even Warren Buffett, considered the greatest investor of all time, recently gave the following instruction for investing his wealth after he dies: "Put 10% of the cash in short-term government bonds and 90% in a very low-cost S&P 500 index fund. . . . I believe that trust's long-term results from this policy will be superior to those attained by most investors—whether pension funds, institutions, or individuals—who employ high-fee managers."[1]

Buffett's advice is on the right track, but my colleagues and I in the evidence-based community go beyond basic index funds to further improve our odds of investment success. And our strategy not only leads to better financial results—it also creates happier, more fulfilled human beings.

I work with successful people who have been poorly served by the conventional investing world. Clients often come to us anxious about the future and saddled with complex, inefficient, and expensive investment portfolios. We offer them a simple, rational, understandable approach and a new sense of freedom. They no longer have to worry about which investments to pick next or where the markets are going, because they have the long-term odds of success on their side.

I know our approach is powerful because I get to see what happens to investors after they make the change. I've witnessed clients proudly hold up their iPhones to show me that they've erased all the stocks they used to obsessively follow, telling me how liberating it feels. I meet with clients who say that their only worry now is how to sink a downhill, sidehill, three-foot putt. I've seen a formerly buttoned-up executive obsessed with controlling the uncontrollable transform into a guy who builds homes for the less fortunate and recently made a list of sixty-five things he'll do in his sixty-fifth year of life.

These life-changing stories are why I love what I do. Seeing how evidence-based investing makes a positive impact on our clients' whole lives—not just their bank accounts—convinces me that we're truly helping people. Now I'm inviting you to learn how evidence-based investing could change your life, just as it has changed my life and the lives of thousands of other investors in the past two decades.

Notes

1David Wismer. "Warren Buffett: 'Investing Advice for You—and My Wife' (and Other Quotes of the Week)," *Forbes*, March 14, 2014.

_____

Chapter 1

WHAT WOULD ALEX KEATON DO?

I don't remember the precise date, but I do remember that it was a Tuesday evening in the fall of 1997. The night was cool and dry, and I was a young man on a mission. I had styled myself with care, and now I stood in front of my bedroom mirror examining the results. I was wearing my only suit, a $700 Calvin Klein number in glen plaid that I'd bought the year before, just after graduating from the University of Missouri.

I thought I looked pretty good. And why not? That suit had cost me every penny of my tax refund. It had been weird to walk into the nicest shop in town and drop that much on a jacket and a pair of pants. I'd felt like I didn't belong in the store, and I certainly hadn't yet accomplished anything to make me worthy of such expensive clothes. But in my mind, the suit wasn't about who I was at the time; it represented who I wanted to be.

As a newly minted college grad, I was expecting my life to start filling up with what I thought of as "really important events." I didn't know what these really important events would look or feel like, but I figured I should be dressed appropriately when they did start happening.

I was pretty sure that this night was going to be a really important event for me, and I wanted to send the message that I knew what was at stake. I cared. I was serious. The suit was already doing its part by giving me a little extra confidence. I took a final look in the mirror—all good—and headed downstairs and out the front door. I climbed into my car, backed out of my parents' driveway, and headed for a date with what I truly hoped would be my destiny.

A few weeks earlier, I had washed up back at my parents' house in Edwardsville, Illinois, after quitting the Saint Louis University School of Law. This was a big deal. I had planned to become a lawyer ever since I was a kid. I'd always thought of lawyers as intellectual warriors, who used logic and charisma to win arguments and help people. When I was growing up in Edwardsville, my family's next-door neighbor was a high-powered defense attorney. Early in the morning, I'd hear the thud of a heavy car door closing, followed by the purr of a Lincoln Town Car gliding away to take him to work or maybe to the airport, on his way to win his next big case. I had visions of growing up and kissing my adoring wife good-bye on the front steps each morning, as my own chauffeur-driven car stood waiting to carry me into battle against the forces of evil.

Barely a month into my first semester at law school, my elaborate fantasies were in tatters. My disillusionment started when all of us first-year students were invited to a lecture by a local legend in the St. Louis legal community. I expected him to congratulate us on our career choice and offer insights that would help us reach the pinnacle of our noble profession. Instead, he dumped a bucket of cold water on every head in the room. He told us that only 10 percent of our class would end up with good jobs at the top law firms. The rest of us, he said, would be left scrounging for scraps.

I was a little taken aback, but my instinct was to shake it off and move on. I've always loved it when people underestimate me. But over the next day or two, another thought kept popping into my head: *I will be $70,000 in debt when I graduate from law school.* Given what our local hero had said, I wasn't sure I liked the odds of landing a good enough job to be able to pay off those loans.

A few days after the lecture, I dropped by my advisor's office to ask him what he thought about my prospects. My advisor was in his late 50s and had been around long enough that he was tired of kids with idealized visions of life as a legal eagle. He told me he agreed that most of us would barely get by after graduating from law school. Then he said, "Do you want to know what the life of a lawyer is really like? Read this."

He handed me a copy of a best-selling nonfiction book called

A Civil Action. The book tells the story of a lawyer pursuing a case against industrial polluters who have poisoned a town's water supply and caused local kids to develop leukemia. The book is 500 pages long. It's well reported and well written, but it's kind of a brutal read if you're thinking of getting into legal work. The lawyer spends the better part of a decade working insane hours on a case that seems likely to go against him. I won't tell you whether he wins the case, but (spoiler alert) I will tell you that the guy ends up bankrupt.

My fantasy of kissing my wife on the way out to the limo each morning was replaced with an image of bankruptcy and divorce. I'd imagined myself helping people solve problems and navigate the legal system, while making a bunch of money in the process. But as I read, I began to picture myself living a life of unbearable stress, with nothing to show for it. That book made me feel like the odds were against me doing much good as a lawyer, no matter how hard I worked. And if the guy in the book couldn't thrive with his off-the-charts dedication and obvious smarts, what made me think I'd do better? Meanwhile, I was borrowing $70,000 to buy my way into this life.

I dropped out of law school the day before my first tuition payment was due.

It was depressing. For the next few weeks, I moped around my parents' house, trying to avoid bumping into them in the kitchen or the hallway. I had fallen short of their expectations, as well as my own. For the first time in my young life, I had tasted failure.

But that night, in my $700 suit, as I pulled away from my parents' driveway, I felt like I was putting that failure behind me. I drove the 30 miles across town to Clayton, a high-end suburb of St. Louis, in a state of total concentration. I didn't even turn on the radio. I needed to focus on the task ahead of me. I needed to convince a bunch of sophisticated and successful grown-ups that I was a smart, hungry kid on his way to big things—not just a law school dropout with no plan B.

My mind wandered to a pep talk my Dad had given me the week before, during lunch at our favorite Chinese restaurant in a not-so-great part of town. Dad was a school principal at the time, and a great listener. He always said that his work taught him that sometimes people need a kick in the ass, and sometimes they need a pat on the butt. I'd turned to him for guidance after walking away from law school, hoping he'd give me a pat on the butt and reassure me that everything was going to be okay. He did more than that: He offered me a path out of what felt like the wreckage of my (admittedly very young) life.

While we shared a plate of garlic chicken, he told me that I needed to stop worrying about success and instead just find a job doing something I love. Then he said, "I know you're passionate about two things: You love financial markets and investments, and you're really into golf. We know that you're not going to win the British Open, so what about finding a job in finance?"

My dad was right. I had always been interested in how money

works. And by the time I'd hit college in the mid-1990s, investing was *cool*. The first Internet bubble was still inflating, and investors thought they could ride hot stocks to instant wealth. The media was full of stories of initial public offerings (IPOs) that doubled or tripled on their first day of trading and then went on to even greater gains.

A couple of guys at school subscribed to *The Wall Street Journal*, which seemed high brow to me. I started reading it just to see what was going on. I was fascinated by what I found: the stories of how companies succeeded and failed, the fortunes being made and lost in various industries, the way events in one part of the world rippled through the global economy. My schoolteacher parents were not *Wall Street Journal* types—they read the *St. Louis Post-Dispatch*—so this was all new to me.

Dad's advice got me thinking. In college, I had discovered a knack for sorting through complex information, identifying themes and connections, and then explaining what was going on in simple, direct ways. I thought this talent would carry me far in a law career. Now I was seeing how financial services could marry my intellectual interests with my idealistic notions of doing something to help other people.

I was seeing how financial services could marry my intellectual interests with my idealistic notions of doing something to help other people.

Investors often struggle to make sense of everything that's going on in the financial markets, which means they have a hard time making good decisions about what to do with their money. I could picture myself diligently studying the markets to learn how they really work, and then explaining it all to investors. Maybe this was my chance to do something worthwhile—and to make some decent money doing it.

A week after that conversation with my Dad, I had what looked like an opportunity to get my life back on the rails. The day after that fateful lunch, I had come across an ad in the *Post-Dispatch* announcing that one of the city's big brokerage firms was looking for candidates for its financial-advisor-in-training program. A training program sounded ideal. I would surround myself with some of the smartest, most successful people in the industry and soak up everything I needed to know to become a successful financial advisor myself. I'd spend my career making everyday people rich, choosing just the right investments at just the right times. I'd earn the respect of other brokers and gain a reputation in the community for doing well by doing good. I'd invent a new model for the 21st-century broker, combining the Zen-like calm of a California surfer with an intense commitment to research and a cosmopolitan worldview—all while living in the heartland of America. I'd still be kissing my future wife every morning on the way out the door to a waiting car. But instead of heading to court, I'd be on my way to make a dazzling presentation to a roomful of wealthy investors.

The ad in the paper invited interested candidates to come to an informational meeting and reception at the brokerage office at 6:00 p.m. on the following Tuesday. I arrived 15 minutes early (there was no way I was going to show up late), parked in the garage, and entered the lobby of the imposing 14-story office tower. I took a second to register how clean and slick the space felt, then crossed the gray-tiled floor to board the elevator that would take me to the brokerage firm's penthouse offices.

When I got to the top floor, the doors slid open to reveal a room that met all of my expectations: dark wood paneling, brass trim on the doors and light fixtures, nice art on the walls. The place had a vibe; it felt masculine, and it radiated success and substance. I got a sense that this company had been around for a long time. Important work happened here. The few people I saw walking through the lobby looked busy, well dressed, and confident. I figured they must be the savvy financial experts who helped investors achieve their goals.

I was greeted by a friendly receptionist sitting at a huge built-in wooden desk. She cheerfully led me to a staircase that took us down to the firm's second floor. We made our way to a conference room, where rows of chairs had been set up classroom style. I was glad I was early, so I could sit in the front row. I wanted to be noticed and to make it clear that I was hungry for what this firm had to offer.

Over the next 10 minutes, I watched as 20 or so other candidates slowly filed into the room. I noticed that they looked like me—mostly young guys in dark suits, white shirts, and conservative ties. They seemed comfortable in their clothes and in this setting, like they had the job already. Maybe they'd gone to Ivy League schools or came from families with long histories in the financial industry. I wasn't rattled, though. I was confident that I could work harder than any of these guys. And given my recent law school flameout, I figured I wanted this opportunity more than any of them did.

The branch manager eventually stood up to welcome us. I was a little taken aback. He reminded me of my old law school advisor. He seemed a little tired, a little burnt out—like he was feigning enthusiasm for the speech he was giving. He said that finance was a great industry, and that this firm was the perfect place to learn the skills we needed to carve out our place in it. His tone wasn't too convincing. But then the branch manager introduced one of the firm's partners to explain the training program to us. It was immediately clear who was the headliner of this event.

The partner looked like . . . a partner. He even *moved* like one, as he strode confidently to the center of the room. He was probably in his 60s, but he seemed young and full of vigor, like one of those guys you see in a Viagra commercial. He was tall and straight-backed, with a full head of perfectly trimmed silver hair. He was dressed flawlessly in a conservative Brooks Brothers suit. This guy simply *radiated* confidence, wisdom, and trustworthiness.

The partner—actually, he seemed more like "The Partner"—stood looking out at us. A slight smile played on his distinguished features as he surveyed the crowd of young applicants, each of us hoping to win a place on the team. He kept us hanging for a minute, giving us some more time to admire him, and then launched into his pitch in the practiced speaking voice of a television or radio professional. His firm was looking for a few bright, young recruits to join a noble calling. We'd learn alongside experts in the art of investing. They'd help us develop our skills so that we could become artists ourselves, empowered to create better futures for our clients. And along the way, we would make an excellent living.

He took half an hour to weave his story and left us wanting to hear more. I took the bait. This firm had just what I needed: status, respectability, and an opportunity to learn a skill and use it to help others. Here some of the smartest financial experts in the world would take me under their wings and teach me how to help my clients and myself.

I felt only one hint of concern beneath my growing excitement: How tough would it be to make the cut for this awesome program? There was a cocktail reception after the presentation. Rather than leave things to chance and risk blending in with all the other young guys in suits, I stood around until I saw a chance to introduce myself to the partner and the branch manager. I wanted them to know that I *wanted* this.

I looked The Partner in the eyes and laid it on the line: "This feels like a great opportunity," I said. "I hope I have what you're looking for."

The two of them exchanged a knowing look that I thought translated along these lines: *This kid gets it. Might just be a keeper. Nice suit, too.*

I was a changed person as I drove back to my parents' house that night. I had the music cranked up and I drummed my fingers to the beat, feeling totally amped up about my future. Things were about to change for me. No one else knew yet, but I was confident I was on my way.

Sure enough, the branch manager called the next day and asked me to come in to the office as soon as possible. We made an appointment for the next morning, and I went in for my formal interview. I don't remember the details all that well, but by then, I was super confident. I felt like we were just going through the motions to make it official. So I wasn't surprised when I got the call that Friday asking me to come into the office Monday morning to start my training.

As soon as I got off the phone, I ran to tell my parents the good news. I could see how relieved they were—not just because I had found a job, but also because I had finally emerged from my post-dropout bout of moping. For my part, I was sure I wouldn't let them down again.

I like weekends, but this one felt like it would never end. When Monday morning finally dawned, I got up, showered, and took my one and only suit out of the closet. I cringed a little at the thought that I would run into at least a few people who would remember it from the week before. *Whatever,* I thought to myself. *I'd be buying more suits soon enough.*

I ran downstairs, wolfed down some toast and a banana, and then ran out to the car with a cup of coffee. This time, I didn't want silence as I drove across town to the office. I punched on the radio but realized I had no idea which station to choose. I remember thinking, *What do capitalists listen to in the morning? What would Alex Keaton listen to on his way to work?* I'd always thought of Alex— the conservative, teenage wannabe-Yuppie son of two former hippies on the '80s television megahit *Family Ties*—as the model of a capitalist. Now, it seemed, he'd become my role model.

Anyway, I figured there had to be a station geared toward important business news and thoughtful market commentary. I couldn't find one, so I kept flipping around. I couldn't listen to pop music or hip-hop; that was kid stuff. I ended up tuned to the easy listening station, which hardly pumped me up, but at least felt like something an adult might like.

The music was kind of awful, to tell you the truth. But it was like the brand-new light-brown leather briefcase sitting on the passenger seat next to me, looking a little out of place, like maybe some friend of my parents had left it there. Both the briefcase and the music served as symbols that something fundamental in me had changed. I didn't have to feel like a law school dropout anymore. I was now one of those people who do real work. *Important* work. *Valuable* work. Work that would make a *difference.*

I woke up from my daydream—so much for staying focused—and there it was. I looked up at the building and tried to identify the 14th floor, where I'd be starting my new life. I thought I could pick it out, but I wasn't sure. I turned into the parking area, where I found a spot easily. I'd been in this garage a few times now. I was already killing it. I stepped out of my car, took a breath, squared my shoulders, gripped the handle of my briefcase a little tighter, and entered the building.

I'd arrived a little early (I wanted to beat the other new recruits), and I could tell that the building was just waking up, getting ready for a busy day. The few people in the lobby were moving slowly. They looked like maybe they needed some caffeine, but I was already buzzing. I nodded to the security guard as I crossed the lobby. I felt conspicuous as I tried to pretend that I'd done this trip hundreds of times before, and reached the elevator feeling like I'd just smuggled something across a border. There were some buttons on the wall in front of me. I pushed one of them, and it illuminated.

The door opened, and I entered it.

I was going up.

Chapter 2

THE BRIEFCASE KID

The first thing that hit me when I walked into the office was the energy level. The place seemed even more jazzed up than I was. About 20 brokers were either sitting or standing at generic, gray workstations in the center of a rectangular room. They were almost all men, dressed conservatively, but quite a few had already ditched their jackets and rolled up their sleeves. The perimeter of the room was lined with glass-walled offices, which I soon learned were reserved for the branch manager and the firm's star brokers. You had to be the best of the best to get an office. Everyone else had to fight it out in the crowded bull pen, where there weren't even enough desks for everyone—least of all us new trainees.

The bull pen was the source of the unmistakable buzz, a compound of low-pitched sound and high-pitched energy that seemed to permeate the place. There was a small speaker on every desk—the squawk box—pumping out the day's stock recommendations from the analysts at the firm's New York headquarters. Scattered here and there were a few televisions tuned to a financial news channel, where talking heads were trying to interpret the signs from the morning's trading session. But no one seemed to be paying attention to those voices, because almost every person in the bull pen was on the phone. I noticed that not a single one of them was listening. They were all talking.

I caught snippets of the chatter as I walked past the rows of workstations. One broker implored a client to get into a stock; another was talking about a new technology company. Meanwhile, assistants ran back and forth between the bull pen and a back room that was hidden behind a wall. I'd later learn that this mysterious room housed the cashiering desk. The runners were carrying paper notes to trigger trades on behalf of the brokers' clients.

I found my way to the branch manager. He led me downstairs to another meeting room, where I sat on a folding chair in a group of 15 or so other trainees. We were told to wait a few minutes for The Partner from the recruiting meeting; he would soon arrive to give us the lowdown on our new job. In the meantime, I looked around at the others. I was kind of surprised at how many people had made the cut. Wasn't I special? Wasn't the *job* special? I shook off those thoughts for the moment and focused on my goal, which was personified by the elegant man who had just walked into the room. I wanted to be like him some day, and I was about to take my first steps in that direction. It was a big moment.

The Partner explained that our job for the next six months was to study for several professional licensing exams. FINRA (the acronym stands for the Financial Industry Regulatory Authority, but no one ever says the name), the governing body that oversees the securities industry, wouldn't let us buy and sell stocks or bonds until we'd passed these exams (Series 7, 63, and 65). Because we couldn't yet work for clients and earn commissions on investment sales, we'd be paid a flat salary of $25,000 for the first year. We'd earn our modest keep by supporting the firm's current brokers. We'd answer the phones and initiate calls for them, listen carefully to their instructions, observe how they did their jobs, and help them with everything else—whether that meant running their trade orders to the cashiering desk or getting them a sandwich. It reminded me of pledging a fraternity: Whatever the brothers needed, you did it for them. In return, you might or might not be invited to stick around.

That's right. There were no guarantees that this was going to work out. On the contrary, The Partner warned that some of us would quit before we even took the test. Others would fail the test, and they'd be done. Out of a job. Goodbye. In fact, the odds of sticking it out were even worse than they sounded. I later learned that the attrition rate is so high for these training programs that brokerage firms have to attract 20 recruits just to fill two positions. I wasn't a handpicked elite candidate; I was cannon fodder.

No wonder The Partner and branch manager exchanged such an odd look when I eagerly introduced myself that night at the reception. They weren't impressed by my commitment; their look was saying something like "Get a load of this one. He really thinks we're that selective?" (My earnest, Alex Keaton–inspired persona would continue to amuse or puzzle these guys during my entire tenure at the firm. Many years later, I heard from a broker who worked there at the time that the firm's big shots—the ones in the offices—called me "the Briefcase Kid" behind my back.)

That first day, I still had no idea how badly I'd misread the situation, but The Partner's speech had planted the first concerns in my head. I'd kind of been hoping for china coffee cups and passionate debates about the role of the stock market in our democracy. But no worries; I'd be fine. I knew that I could outwork and outstudy anyone. And once I understood the fundamentals of the financial markets, my natural curiosity would help me analyze trends and identify great investments for clients.

But the day wasn't over yet. That afternoon, I had an even more jarring experience. I was making my way around the offices on the perimeter of the bull pen, trying to introduce myself to the firm's top brokers and partners. Most weren't there or were too busy to be bothered, but I came across one partner who seemed approachable and eager to talk. He was a short, round, jolly guy in his late 50s. I introduced myself, and we chatted for a few minutes. I liked him right away and said something about how I was eager to learn what he could teach me about finding good investments. Just then, we were interrupted by a young broker who had come stomping over from the bull pen. I didn't know it yet, but this broker was one of the jolly partner's closest associates, and he was not happy to see some newbie trying to work his way into the partner's good graces. The young broker saw me

Then he said, "Make no mistake, kid. You're a salesman, not an analyst."

as a potential threat to his own ascent through the firm's ranks, and he quickly ended my cordial conversation with the jolly partner by making up some task for me to do back in the bull pen.

As we walked back among the workstations, the young broker started telling me that I was too new to really understand how things worked. Then he said, "Make no mistake, kid. You're a salesman, not an analyst."

I was confused. I didn't like the sound of his pronouncement, but I shook off the doubts that crept into my mind. *Maybe that's how some people see this job*, I thought, *but not me*. I resolved to keep my head down and continue to learn.

And learn I did. One of my early jobs was creating and distributing the daily "blotter" for all the brokers. This one-page report collected important headlines from publications like *The New York Times, The Wall Street Journal, Barron's, The Financial Times, Investor's Business Daily*, and *The Bond Buyer*. Each morning, I'd spend half an hour scanning such publications in search of news that might help our brokers help their clients. I was told to look for at least one big story about stocks, one about bonds, and something that seemed important on a global or macroeconomic level. When I found a good story, I'd cut the headline and the first paragraph or two out of the paper and paste the clippings on either side of a sheet of paper. Then, I'd photocopy this handmade newsletter and distribute it to everyone in the office.

It never occurred to me to wonder why they'd trust a total neo-phyte with the task of deciding which stories were important and which weren't. All I knew was that I had a job to do; and man, I took it seriously. I chose the stories with exquisite care, in the belief that the brokers would appreciate my efforts and put them to good use on behalf of their clients. What I liked even more was the social aspect of the job: I could get to know the success-ful brokers because I had to pop into their offices every morning. Whether they liked it or not, seeing my all-too-eager face was now a regular part of their day.

After a few mornings on blotter duty, I happened to notice one of the top brokers grab the paper off his desk. His eyes went imme-diately to the bottom of the front page. He frowned, crumpled the blotter, and threw it in the trash. I thought, *Wow, what an insult! Doesn't he appreciate how carefully I've selected this collection of stories? He must be having a tough day!*

But it was strange, so I started paying closer attention to the brokers' reactions when I dropped off the blotter. That's when I noticed the same little scene unfolding again and again as I walked down the row of offices along the perimeter of the room. The broker would pick up the blotter, his eyes would dart to the lower corner of the page, and then he'd toss the thing in the trash. There was only one variation: Some guys would smile before they threw the blotter away; others would frown.

What was so fascinating about the bottom of the blotter? There was an easy answer. The firm chose that spot—the lower right-hand corner, to be exact—to list every broker's production numbers from the day before. "Production" translated to the amount of money the broker earned for the firm (not for the clients, mind you). If you had sold a lot of stocks or bonds the day before and earned a lot of commissions for the firm, you'd show up as a top producer. If you hadn't . . . well, your name would be way down on the list.

I became upset when I figured that out. I might not have minded so much if they'd at least read the pieces I clipped out for them every morning—pieces I thought were there to help them make money for their clients. But they made a joke out of the rest of the blotter by just trashing it. I started to wonder whether all my carefully chosen articles and the news and insights they offered were just window dressing for the information that really mattered: how much money the brokers were making for themselves.

Still, I thought maybe I'd misread the situation. I began to investigate. I'd walk into a broker's office and say something like, "Hey, did you read that story about energy stocks in the blotter today?"

They'd get this perplexed look on their face. I'm sure they were thinking something like *Great, what's the Briefcase Kid doing here? How can I get him to scram?* They'd mutter something about having to make a call, and shoo me away.

Even this didn't discourage me—not at first. I'd just move on to the next person. Meanwhile, I made excuses for my colleagues' seeming obsession with production numbers. After all, these guys worked for a major Wall Street firm. Of *course* they wanted to make money. That didn't mean they didn't care about their clients. It just made them more motivated to do a good job.

Remember, I was only 25 years old and maybe a little naïve, even for my age. But that was starting to change—and there was much more to come.

Chapter 3

WOLVES

One month after I arrived at the firm, I was assigned to work with a broker named Mr. P. Trainees rotated through the different brokers, taking turns serving as their assistants. But Mr. P was famous. Even I knew that he was a star, one of the firm's biggest producers. And now I'd be his right-hand man for a week.

What a chance to prove myself! What an opportunity to learn more about the investing business! I can say without the slightest exaggeration that l was thrilled at the prospect.

Mr. P seemed to have the secret to success. He didn't show up at the office until after 10 o'clock every morning, and he was done by two o'clock every afternoon. Somehow, in that four-hour window, he found time to go out to lunch. Meanwhile, he made enough money to drive a fancy car and live in one of the nicest suburbs of

St. Louis. Whatever it was that he knew, my fellow trainees and I were *dying* to know it ourselves.

At the same time, Mr. P scared us. He was hardly a physically imposing person: just an average-sized, balding, middle-aged guy. But he lived his few hours in the office each day with a blazing intensity. He never made small talk and rarely smiled. He glared at everyone who passed his door, warning them against coming any closer, let alone interrupting him.

We had it easy compared with his clients. He never used phone calls as a chance for a friendly chat. No way. We heard him *scream* at clients every day. He'd call an investor to tell the guy which stock he was planning to buy or sell for him. If the investor didn't immediately agree to this plan, Mr. P would attack him. That's the word for it: He'd *attack* the client on the other end of the line, pummeling him with verbal jabs until he saw the chance to deliver a devastating uppercut for the knockout blow. The monologue might go something like this: "Do you pay me to make decisions for you or not? Do you want to go back to making decisions for yourself? What's your job? You're a lawyer, right? Well, I'm a professional investor! Go back to lawyering, and leave the investing decisions to me!"

His tone was withering, and he was incredibly loud. Heaven forbid the poor guy on the other end put up further resistance, because eventually Mr. P would explode: "This is what we're doing. Call me when you pull your head out of your . . ." and the phone would go down with a SLAM.

So while I believed Mr. P had a lot to teach me about the world of investing, I was a little worried when I took my post at the tiny desk just outside his door. I was afraid I'd do something to make him mad at me. I wasn't allowed in his office, which was fine. I was scared to go in there anyway. But he left the door open. There was also a little sliding window in the wall between us, and he'd occasionally shove paper order tickets through it. I was supposed to take the tickets to the cashiering desk so they could execute his trades. The open door and the little window made it easy to listen in on his routine.

"Matt," he'd say, "get me Paul Johnson on the phone."

I'd dial the client's number, transfer the call into Mr. P's office, then listen while Mr. P "explained" the trades he intended to make on the client's behalf. If the client agreed, Mr. P would be calm and encouraging. He'd say, "Super. I believe this is going to be a great move. We're doing it with all our best clients, and you're certainly one of the smartest people I work with. This is going to work out really well for you . . . "

But if the client asked questions or hesitated, Mr. P would erupt. I remember a particularly bad explosion one afternoon. Mr. P had been calling his clients all morning, telling them he was moving everyone out of Coke and into Pepsi. One of the last guys he called must have had a question about the fees he would pay for the trade, because Mr. P went through the roof. It was the loudest I'd ever heard him scream at anyone. He acted as if he had never been so insulted in all his life. "Am I really hearing this? Are you actually questioning my integrity? How dare you! You've got some kind of nerve after all I've done for you!"

He had an extra-long phone cord so he could pace in front of his window while making calls. The tirade went on and on, until I heard the telltale slam of the phone. I gathered my courage and stuck my head in his door to ask if everything was okay.

Mr. P seemed just fine. He was standing there, staring down at the street below. In fact, I'd rarely seen him in such a good mood. With the air of a general who has just eaten an excellent meal and is now speaking to an inferior who hasn't done anything to annoy him lately, he said to me, "Don't worry, Matt. This happens from time to time. But it's why I try to find the right clients."

He looked at me for a beat. "Matt, do you know how I like my clients?"

"Um, no, Mr. P."

He continued to eye me with an air of vaguely terrifying benevolence. "Would you like me to *tell* you how I like my clients?"

"Um, sure, Mr. P. Absolutely."

"Rich and dumb," said Mr. P.

He seemed to savor the words as he slowly repeated them. "That's how I like them. Rich. And. Dumb."

I had actually picked up a notebook to write down whatever gem he was going to offer. Granted, taking notes also meant I wouldn't have to look him in the face, which was always a little nerve-racking. But at those last three words I stopped writing and looked up at him. I was confused, but I was fascinated, too. He didn't seem finished.

"People who are rich and dumb *delegate*," he explained. "They know they don't know anything about this stuff, and they know that I do. They *don't ask questions*."

And with that, Mr. P turned back to his desk, sat down, and asked me to get another client on the phone. I realized my lesson was over. I left the room in a daze. Had he really said what I thought he had just said?

As my week in the service of Mr. P continued, I realized that his emotional eruptions were an act. Whenever he encountered anyone too independent minded to accept his suggestions without comment, he simply flipped on his alpha dog switch and browbeat them into submission. His idea of providing investment guidance was to scare the hell out of people.

For a time, I tried to tell myself that maybe his approach was defensible. After all, Mr. P was a professional investor who (presumably) knew what he was doing. His clients were amateurs. Maybe Mr. P was right to force his (presumably) brilliant investment ideas on them.

Still, it bothered me. Shouldn't clients be allowed to ask questions? Why didn't he want a discussion? Was he just in a hurry to dole out more brilliant ideas? Or, and this was a troubling thought, was he afraid that he couldn't answer the questions? What if he wasn't such an expert after all? How much did he really know about the stocks he was selling?

This line of thought led me to an even more troubling question: Did Mr. P even *care*? Did he really have his clients' best interests at heart? If anything, he seemed to hold his clients in contempt. What if he wanted the clients to shut up so that he could do whatever he wanted, whether or not it was in their best interest? Mr. P made a commission every time he bullied, coaxed, or otherwise manipulated a client into buying or selling some stock. Back then, clients were paying $300 to $500 for a big trade, so moving 100 clients a day into or out of the same stock allowed the firm—and Mr. P—to pocket thousands of dollars. Maybe what he was really thinking when he was yelling at his client was *Make the damn trade so I can hang up and collect my commission.*

It was a horrible thought. Part of me still wasn't quite ready to go there. Maybe Mr. P meant well. Maybe he really did know what he was talking about, and maybe he was trying to help clients. Maybe he was even succeeding. I wasn't totally sure of anything at this point. But I did know that I didn't want to be like him, screaming at clients and making snide remarks about them to younger colleagues.

And so, having abandoned one role model, I went looking for another. My next candidate was Mr. J, a weathered old trader who seemed to have been around forever. He looked like an even crustier Jeff Bridges, and he was probably the calmest guy in the building—maybe because he sold bonds, not stocks. Also in sharp contrast to Mr. P, Mr. J was always in the office. If I showed up at the crack of dawn, he'd already be at his desk, sipping coffee. And no matter how late I left at the end of the day, he'd still be there. I never heard him talking to clients on the phone, let alone screaming at them, and he never seemed to be busy. Yet he was consistently ranked with Mr. P among the firm's top producers.

He was always friendly to me when I dropped off the blotter, and I noticed that he actually glanced at a few things on it besides the production numbers before throwing it away. So I felt comfortable walking into Mr J's office one day and asking if he would me tell me his story. I mentioned that he seemed to approach the job differently from everyone else, and that I would love to hear the secret of his success.

As with most of the firm's big brokers, it wasn't hard to get him talking about himself. They didn't see me as a threat, and I think my interest flattered them. "You really want to know?" he said. "I'll tell you. Just become a fixed-income expert and sell bonds to big institutions or wealthy individuals. There's no way you can fail."

"Why is that, Mr. J?"

He smiled a knowing smile and said, "Because no one knows how much we pay for the bonds."

He paused, while I looked at him blankly. Then, seeing that I didn't get it, he continued, "Clients want bonds, and we have bonds to sell. But since they don't know how much we pay for those bonds, they don't know how much we mark the prices up when we sell them. Our clients don't know what we're really charging them, so no one ever complains."

Today, I actually admire his honesty—no one else at the firm would speak that directly about what was going on. At the time, I was deflated by the revelation. I'd come to this job expecting to join a team that would do everything it could to help people discover winning investments. I was starting to wonder whether I was just part of a gang of white-collar thugs who were fleecing clients at every opportunity. Some fleeced clients quietly, and some did it loudly, almost violently. But regardless of style differences, the primary motivation behind every action appeared to be turning clients upside down and shaking money out of their pockets.

I was starting to wonder whether I was just part of a gang of white-collar thugs who were fleecing clients at every opportunity.

I still clung to the fading hope that things weren't as bad as I thought. In a way, I was right: They were worse.

I started paying attention to the squawk box on every broker's desk. Each day, the disembodied voices of the firm's New York–based analysts would announce that such and such stock was a strong buy. The brokers would then call up their clients to tell them about this exciting new opportunity, even though the brokers actually knew very little about the stock.

Maybe the brokers' ignorance would have been okay (not ideal, but at least a little less distressing) if the *analysts* were investment geniuses toiling to make clients rich. In that case, the brokers' role was simply to pass the analysts' wonderful ideas along to the clients.

Nope, the analysts weren't on the clients' side either. They were getting paid to come up with ideas that would generate trades. That often meant focusing on a splashy story rather than looking for the best long-term value out there. And there were other conflicts of interest. If an analyst wrote something negative about a stock, the company would stop taking his calls, making it impossible for him to do his (highly compensated) work. Meanwhile, the firm's investment banking division didn't want analysts to say anything that could jeopardize their chances of landing lucrative banking deals from the companies that analysts covered. Bottom line: The analysts couldn't say what they really believed about a firm and the value of its stock.

I didn't fully understand all of this back then, but the analysts' role still struck me as weird. Every few months, the firm's analysts would visit our office to make presentations that were more like pep rallies. You'd get one guy pumping you up about the Dow hitting 10,000 (back when it was around 8,000), then another guy touting his list of the 10 best stocks to buy next month. It was a little like a coach giving a rousing locker room speech before the big game.

The analyst always seemed like a believer, and he made you want to believe right along with him. The brokers would get energized about an investment idea and take that energy right back to their desks, where they would immediately start calling clients with the pitch. Not once did I hear anyone question the latest idea or ask whether it made sense for a particular client's portfolio. That sort of thing wasn't an issue.

By now, I was ready to admit that the client's interests were at best a secondary concern for the brokers, who simply wanted to land at or near the top of the firm's production numbers each morning. Meanwhile, the firm was happy to charge clients ridiculous fees for the privilege of having their interests largely ignored. What was worse, the markups on each trade crippled the clients' investment returns.

I told myself that maybe those costs could be justified if the firm was delivering amazing performance for its clients. But the firm's investment results weren't anything special, as far as I could tell. If they had been, believe me, someone would have been bragging about it. As it was, no one seemed to care how clients' portfolios were doing. The brokers almost never talked about it.

Adding injury to injury, they never stopped to think about the tax implications of the trades they were making. Would the client face a big capital gain on a trade? Would the trade create a loss they could use on their tax returns the next year? That was the client's problem, because it didn't affect the brokers' commissions in any way.

I figured that if you took care of your customers, you'd succeed. But no one at this firm thought that way. They thought about increasing their own income, and everything else was irrelevant.

Clearly, there was a problem here. And as I would soon realize, the problem extended way beyond the confines of our office in Clayton, Missouri.

Chapter 4

A BROKEN MODEL

I began to wander around the office in a state of mild shock. I found myself more and more confused. Two major questions kept running through my mind: First, how could these guys act this way? Second, why were their clients putting up with such lousy treatment?

My initial thought when pondering the first question was that I'd just happened to fall in with a den of thieves. In fact, that would have been much easier to accept than the truth that was gradually emerging: Most of these brokers weren't terrible human beings. They were decent people trapped in a terrible business model.

My employer, like other Wall Street firms, was designed to do one thing: Make as much money as possible . . . for itself. Typically, that meant accumulating as many clients as possible (preferably rich and dumb), managing as much of their money as possible, and then generating a flurry of investment activity that created massive commissions and fees for the firm—even if that didn't necessarily add up to value for the client.

That's why brokers were so worried about their production numbers. In just a few hours, a guy like Mr. P could churn 50 of his clients out of one stock and into another, earn a $300 commission on every trade, and knock off for the afternoon. He'd had a good day. His clients? Who knew? Who cared, really?

The job was selling. Even the analysts were basically glorified salespeople, whose main job was to generate excitement over a particular investment. As for the brokers, they weren't going to question the analysts' picks, let alone come up with their own investment ideas. And they certainly weren't going to spend much time, if any, worrying about which investments were suitable for a particular client. That sort of thing would have cut into their selling time, undermining their shot at becoming one of the firm's top producers and reaping the accompanying rewards.

Wall Street's model made sure that those rewards were pretty tempting. For starters, you got paid a piece of the fees you generated for the firm. Star performers could work out a bigger cut, along with perks like a bigger office, an executive parking space, and more assistants. Then, there were the contests: You could win a trip to Hawaii for selling the most bonds in a month or get sent to a luxury resort on the Caribbean island of Nevis for getting the most clients into one of the firm's proprietary mutual funds.

Even so, the carrot wasn't as big a motivator as the stick. There was no such thing as tenure in this business. A few bad months and they'd take away that big office and the good parking space. A few more bad months and they'd take away your job.

I once asked the branch manager to describe the ideal broker, assuming I'd get some ideas about how to succeed. His answer: He wanted someone who was a successful salesman, but was *leveraged to the hilt*. He wanted his guys to own huge houses, drive fancy cars, and put their kids in private schools. That way, they'd never be able to leave. They'd also be terrified to let their production slip, since that would mean giving up their lifestyle. The branch manager (who was under similar pressure) used the production figures in the blotter to turn up the competition among the brokers.

I started noticing brokers whose careers were in trouble. You'd see a guy sitting at his desk with his head in his hands, poring over the client lists of the brokers who had recently left the firm, hoping to find new names for his roster. You'd see people staying late at night, making cold calls with increasing desperation. You could see fear in their eyes—they were like wounded animals being edged out of the pack. Sometimes, they'd try underhanded tactics in the fight for their survival, like asking the branch manager to route another broker's incoming calls to them instead. And then, one day, the weak producer would be gone.

This high-stakes competition helped explain why there was absolutely no sharing of ideas among the brokers. No one sat around discussing how the markets worked or why certain investments made better sense for one type of client versus another. The brokers saw their job as a zero-sum game. If you shared a secret with a colleague, that broker would use it to improve his results, which would make you look worse by comparison.

Because the brokers were under such tremendous pressure to make their quotas, they couldn't afford to slow down, identify appropriate investments for each client, and steer their people away from trades that weren't right for them. The firm wouldn't let them. So that answered my first question: I was beginning to understand why the brokers behaved so dishonestly.

My second question was harder to answer: Why did the clients accept this? Why did they allow their brokers to bully them into paying exorbitant commissions for trades that typically didn't make a lot of sense? Why weren't they asking more questions about their brokers' investment ideas? Why didn't they demand better investment results?

I didn't really understand the complex forces at work here (although I'd learn much more about them later). But I did notice one thing that seemed relevant: As with Mr. J's hidden bond markups, the firm worked hard to keep their clients in the dark about everything, including how the firm chose investments, how those investments performed, and how much the firm charged in fees. You've heard of a culture of transparency? This was a culture of opacity.

For starters, the firm never reported a client's performance as a percentage gain or loss that could be measured against an appropriate standard (known as a *benchmark*), such as the S&P 500. Instead, they'd just report results in dollar figures. As long as the market was going up, people tended to make money. But they had no easy way of seeing whether their results were trailing the market's overall returns, so they didn't complain when they earned far less than they could have earned with a better investment mix and more reasonable fees. And if the market went down and the clients' investments lost value, you could just tell them that it was the market's fault, without revealing that their account had fallen even further than the market as a whole.

The firm was also really good at hiding the fees they charged. A client would rarely notice the commission on a stock trade, and no one went to any pains to point it out. Meanwhile, Mr. J had built his whole career on the ability to price bonds way higher than the firm's cost, without ever telling the client. Clients thought Mr. J was doing their bond trades for free. What they didn't realize was that he didn't have to charge them a transaction fee because the price of the bond was already marked up between 2% and 6%. A $100,000 bond trade would automatically create a $2,000 to $6,000 commission for the firm.

Mutual fund investors had even more layers to peel back. As part of my training, I learned that mutual fund companies charged management fees and operating expenses that could range from about 1% to 2% per year. Meanwhile, investors often paid commissions when their brokers bought or sold them shares in a fund, further reducing their potential returns. The size of those fees and commissions typically depended on the "class" of shares that an investor bought. A fund might have A-, B-, and C-class shares, but the only difference between them was in how they charged investors. Some shares had high up-front fees that covered the broker's commission. Some shares charged a fee when investors sold their shares. Some fund shares required investors to hold on to their stake for a certain period of time to avoid paying certain fees (or to qualify for lower fees).

Most brokers would simply pick the shares that paid them the best commissions, and then figure out how to convince the investor that the fund would make him lots of money. Big mutual fund companies would visit our office regularly to hold lunch meetings with the brokers in hopes of getting them to pick *their* funds for our clients. The first question from a broker, inevitably, was "How do we get paid?"

The jolly partner I met with on my first day in the office was an expert at using mutual fund commissions to boost his production. He was actually one of the more enlightened guys that I worked with. He had his Certified Financial Planner designation, which meant that he'd taken courses intended to help him focus on his clients' needs and goals. And he did try to serve his clients well by creating diversified portfolios with a mix of mutual funds that invested in different types of stocks. But he always made sure to pick the mutual funds and class shares that paid him the most. Far be it from him to explain to his clients the difference between an A share and a C share or how that difference affected their costs or his income.

Sure enough, the jolly partner showed up on the blotter as the firm's top producer every time mutual fund companies paid out their monthly or quarterly commissions to brokers. The rest of the time, he didn't crack the top 10, but that didn't bother him. He knew when his paydays were coming.

My colleagues were not doing anything illegal, at least as far as I know. By law, these guys didn't have to act in their clients' best interests or place those interests above their own. FINRA regulations simply required them to be reasonably sure that an investment was "suitable" for a client. No one knew exactly what this meant, but in truth, you had to do something pretty insane for anyone to take notice—like putting all of a 90-year-old woman's retirement savings in shares of a single technology start-up (believe me, it's been done). Nowhere was it written that you couldn't put someone in a dog of an investment that paid a great commission.

After a few months of watching this dysfunctional dance between brokers and their clients, I was starting to feel embarrassed that I'd been conned by the flashy sales pitch at that first recruitment meeting. I was ashamed at what my parents would say if I told them what I was learning. They're both educators who have spent their lives helping others, without worrying unduly about the financial payoff. Yet here I was trying to join an industry where making money for yourself was the only motivation.

During that period, I'd go back to my parents' house at night and study for my exams just to distract myself from the reality of the situation. I kept thinking about the warning I'd received my first day: I was being groomed for a sales job. I'd been naive enough to believe that I was on track to make a real difference in people's lives and that I was joining a group who shared that vision. Some nights, I'd try to imagine how I could challenge the system or invent a way to forge an honorable path through this dishonorable world. But I could never come up with a realistic solution. I grew more and more depressed about my future.

My fellow trainees didn't seem as troubled as I was, but they were all so focused on passing the tests that I never really got a chance to talk with them about the big picture. They didn't seem to care as much as I did about trying to learn from the older brokers or finding mentors. They were more worried about keeping their jobs. Anything that didn't prep them for the tests was just a distraction.

I'd been naive enough to believe that I was on track to make a real difference in people's lives and that I was joining a group who shared that vision.

I eventually discovered that I wasn't the only person at the firm who saw what was going on. The folks in the back office, who processed the trades and handled account records, thought the place was just as screwed up as I did. But they earned a flat salary, and they weren't involved in selling to clients.

I'd wander back to the cashiering desk and float little trial balloons like, "Does anyone around here ever wonder if these brokers have any idea what they're doing?" The women back there (they were mostly women) would laugh and say something along the lines of, "What was your first clue?"

Another time, I might point out that the only questions the brokers asked at the latest mutual fund presentation concerned how much they were going to get paid to sell shares of the fund. The back office crew would hear me out and shake their heads, and someone would say, "I know. It's crazy."

Pretty soon, I realized that the only time I felt normal at work was when I was talking with this group of nonbelievers. These were the folks who had seen behind the curtain, and they had no illusions about what this firm was really doing to its clients. They could afford to admit the truth, unlike the folks who worked in the broker's bull pen.

After three months at the firm, I knew I couldn't stick around for much longer. I kept thinking about the way things could—should—have been. I thought brokers should work hard to find great investment ideas for their clients. They should put clients' interests first. That approach would be good for the brokers, too. Happy clients would become long-term clients and would probably recommend their brokers to their friends and family. I also thought clients should be more engaged. Ideally, they'd ask their brokers lots of intelligent questions. They'd ask why certain investments made sense for them, and they'd want a clear idea of the risks they were facing. I'd pictured long meetings where brokers and clients would discuss the relative merits of IBM and Microsoft shares. I'd imagined myself gently explaining the facts to grateful clients, who would rely on my sage advice to choose winning investments.

In fact, I'd assumed that my main purpose as a stockbroker would be . . . to *help* people.

Clearly, I was in the wrong place. But I still believed—I hoped—that, somewhere, financial professionals actually cared about their clients and actually helped them make good financial decisions. I imagined that those professionals spent their time getting to know the clients, evaluating their circumstances, identifying important goals, and choosing the best investments to meet those goals. I believed there must be people who could pick great stocks or mutual funds and who knew exactly the right time to get in and out of those investments. Their combination of skill, virtue, and hard work would help them succeed most of the time.

It was a powerful vision. But it was a fantasy—at least in part.

But I still believed—I hoped—that, somewhere, financial professionals actually cared about their clients and actually helped them make good financial decisions.

Certainly it would have been nice if the brokers at my firm stopped churning people's accounts and charging them bloated fees. And it would have been a relief to see the brokers treat their clients as human beings with unique needs. But the hard truth was this: *It didn't much matter whether my colleagues tried to pick winners for their clients.*

The idea that hard-working and intelligent professional investors could consistently choose winning stocks, mutual funds, or other individual investments was more or less a sham.

I just didn't know it yet.

Chapter 5

MY LUCK TURNS IN VEGAS

I never really understood why the NCAA Basketball Tournament was called "March Madness" until I experienced it in Las Vegas. That's exactly where I was in the spring of 1999, and it was *crazy*.

Forget Alex Keaton. Picture me in jeans and a polo shirt, downstairs at the Treasure Island Casino on the Strip, having one of the greatest times of my life. I've placed about 10 bets on various teams, and now I'm in the sports book room, watching the games play out, which I can do on a movie theater–sized screen or on one of dozens of TVs stationed around the room. The place is packed with a motley mix of rabid fans in their college sweatshirts, hard-core gamblers, and tourists. Some of them are getting into it, like I am, and others look curious and maybe a little bewildered. It's loud, it's smoky, and it's boozy; it reminds me of a big college party. Most of us are living and dying on every free throw. So far, my picks are doing pretty well. I'm high-fiving and hugging strangers, jumping up and down, and generally feeling fantastic.

This trip is exactly what I needed.

I'd flown to Vegas the night before for a long weekend with my girlfriend, Lisa. The idea was to have fun after my last miserable few months. I'd stuck it out at the brokerage firm for a little more than six months—long enough to pass the Series 7 exam, which qualified me to sell securities. At that point, I was one of five survivors from my class of 15 trainees, so I guess I was supposed to feel like a winner or something. But the closer I came to becoming an actual broker, the more the prospect depressed me. I would look around the office and ask myself whether I really wanted to be here in another year . . . or two . . . or five. Did I really want to join this club?

The answer was an emphatic *no*, but it was tough to admit that to myself. The fact that I had loved studying for the Series 7 exam didn't make my decision any easier. Financial markets still fascinated me, and I was enthralled by the idea of helping people make a better life for themselves by putting their hard-earned money to work in good investments. But the brokers I'd met didn't share that vision, to put it mildly.

I decided I'd rather fail than become a success on their terms. For a while, though, I couldn't bring myself to leave. I felt like I was getting way too good at quitting things, and I couldn't face disappointing my parents again. I imagined them having to make lame excuses for me whenever their friends asked how I was doing. *Oh, he's in transition right now* . . . But, I also knew that, in the long run, they really didn't care how much money I made or what kind of status I achieved. They were more concerned that I take responsibility for myself and make a positive contribution to society.

Then, one day, I was doing the blotter again, thinking about what a joke it was, and suddenly, it came to me: *I am not going to do this anymore.* It scared me to think about what that meant. But I knew in my bones that quitting was my only option.

I walked into the branch manager's office, stood in front of his desk, and laid it on the line. I didn't even have it in me to be tactful. I just said, "This isn't for me. I can't find anybody here who is really thinking about how to serve the client. It feels like it is always about the same thing: 'How do we get paid?'"

He seemed taken aback by my candor—and a little peeved. But he made one last play. He spoke in a gentle, disappointed tone. "Matt," he said, "I really thought you were going to be the one who made it."

Even then, as young and as eager as I was for approval from my elders, I didn't take that as a compliment. And I was done playing the good soldier. I told him, "I will make it. Just not here."

I meant it, too. I hadn't given up on financial services. I still hoped I could make a good living in the investment business while making a difference in people's lives.

The branch manager could tell from my tone and the look on

my face that I was serious; I was actually heading out the door, and I was not coming back. His attitude changed. He wasn't just disappointed; he was angry at me, and he didn't try to hide it. His boss, presumably, wanted at least a few of us to stick around, and now one of the handful of survivors was leaving.

I hadn't given up on financial services. I still hoped I could make a good living in the investment business while making a difference in people's lives.

The next words out of the branch manager's mouth were a threat: "We paid for you to get your securities licenses, and you still owe us. You haven't even started earning money for the firm yet. We'll sue you if you go to another brokerage firm."

I brushed off his warning. I just wanted to get out of there. I said, "I'm sorry it didn't work out," and left. In fact, I bolted. I imagine at least a couple of the big brokers saw me flying out the door and wondered, *Where's the Briefcase Kid going in such a rush?*

I didn't care what they thought; I felt liberated. I had escaped from the trap that had caught them when they were my age. I was so relieved that I didn't give much thought to the branch manager's threat until a few days later.

I was still in bed when I heard the phone ring downstairs at my parents' house. I got up to answer it and soon found myself the central figure in an odd scene: I was standing in my pajamas, getting grilled by a lawyer in New York City, who had called on behalf of my former employer. He started his interrogation by saying, "It looks like you're trying to go to another firm. Is that right?" The question struck me as absurd. I had no such plans. I think I laughed out loud before telling him, no, that was not on my agenda. He then repeated my branch manager's threat: The firm had paid for my training, and I still owed them. They would sue me, or another firm, for those costs if I tried to get another job in the securities industry.

I wasn't quite sure what to make of the situation. It seemed unbelievable, but it made me wonder. Maybe getting another job in financial services wasn't an option. I was already starting to come down from the high I'd experienced upon quitting. I'd escaped, but I was also back where I'd started when I'd dropped out of law school the year before. Maybe I'd learned a thing or two—I was a little less naive about what went on out there in the real world—but I still didn't know what to do with myself.

My parents weren't happy with me, either. They had high expectations for me, and while they weren't pushing me into any particular career, they weren't going to let me just sit around their house trying to figure out what to do next. So this time, instead of a pep talk, they gave me the kick in the ass. About a month after I quit the brokerage firm, they told me to move out of their house. They owned a rental property that was vacant at the time, and they strongly suggested that I move in there and start fixing the place up to earn my keep. Oh, and they wanted me to pay a security deposit, as if I was some random renter off the street! I found this shocking, but the message they sent was clear: I had to get my act together.

So that's what I was doing in Vegas. No, not getting my act together. I was trying to escape my predicament for a few days. It was a huge relief to be away from St. Louis, completely absorbed in March Madness. For those few hours, I didn't have to feel bad about the fact that, at age 25, I'd already failed at two careers and had basically been kicked out of my parents' house. For what felt like the first time in years, I wasn't worried about my future at all. The only things that mattered were whether Missouri State was ahead of Wisconsin and, if so, by how many points. The guy next to me was my best friend for the moment—and the moment was all that counted.

Then, I saw my girlfriend, Lisa. We'd met in college, standing in line at the University of Missouri bookstore. It was the start of the semester, and the line to buy textbooks stretched well out the door. It was obvious we were going to be standing next to each other for a while, so I struck up a conversation. We had been together ever since. Normally, I was glad to see Lisa. On this occasion, not so much. I was perfectly happy on my own. Worse, she looked mad at me. And so she was. Lisa walked up and looked at me with her brown eyes and uttered the following buzz-killing words: "You need to go upstairs and take a shower. We're meeting Dorette and Ed Goldberg for lunch in 45 minutes."

The joy died in my chest. It wasn't that I had a problem with the

Goldbergs. Like us, they were from St. Louis, and they happened to be in Las Vegas for a golf vacation. But I didn't even know them. Lisa and Dorette worked together at Banana Republic, where they had taken part-time jobs mainly to get the employee discount on clothing. Beyond that, Lisa and I didn't seem to have much in common with Dorette and her husband. We were in our 20s; they were in their 50s. I was sure they'd be perfectly nice, but I dreaded the idea of yet another awkward conversation about what I was doing with my life, especially with people who were about the same age as my parents.

I looked at Lisa and made a desperate stab at saving my afternoon. "We all live in St. Louis," I pointed out. "Why don't we just have dinner together when we get home? I *really* need to watch the end of this game. Besides, if I have to shower and get dressed, I'll never make it in time."

She looked back at me. "Oh, yes you will," she said evenly. Clearly, the day's itinerary was not up for debate. Stalling, I asked where we were going for lunch. She told me they'd picked the Cheesecake Factory. I couldn't believe it. I'd been to plenty of malls and eaten in my share of Cheesecake Factories in the past. We were in Vegas, a place with amazing restaurants, but were we going to eat at one of them? We were not. Instead, we were about to meet an older couple from St. Louis, in a chain restaurant—one that had a perfectly good location just down the road from where we all lived back in Missouri. This was absolutely *brutal*.

"You've got to be kidding me," I said. "Why don't we go some-place special?"

But she was done with the conversation. "Just do this," she said. "And don't embarrass me."

An hour later, freshly showered and dressed slightly more neatly in a button-down shirt and khakis, I was sitting next to Lisa and across from Ed and Dorette at the Cheesecake Factory in the mall next to Ceasar's Palace. The decor was a mix of faux-Roman archi-tecture, garish Vegas neon, and generic chain-restaurant style. I tried to ignore my surroundings by focusing on the couple across from me.

The Goldbergs are proof of the old adage that opposites attract. Ed is reserved and serious. Dorette is small and bubbly, friendly and outgoing. I could see why Lisa liked spending time with her. The two of them were immediately in their own world, chatting about work and what they had been doing in Vegas. That left Ed and me to strike up a conversation.

My job status came up almost immediately. Of course.

"I hear you're in financial services," said Ed.

Uh oh, I thought. *Just how much had he heard?*

"I am too," he continued. "I'm part of a small advisory firm in St. Louis."

This surprised me. Ed seemed nothing like the brokers I knew. He wasn't a master of seduction like the recruiter for my previous firm, and I couldn't imagine him laying a hard sell on anyone the way Mr. P did.

I asked him to tell me about his firm. He told me he worked for Buckingham Asset Management, which had only been around for a few years. Then he said, "You know, one of our partners just wrote a book about investing. If you'd like, I'll send you a copy when we get back to St. Louis."

It sounded like a good way to get out of the conversation without discussing my failures. "Sure, sounds good," I said. We moved on to safe topics for guys to talk about: basketball, golf, our families. We had a pretty nice time.

I rushed back to the sports room in time for a few more hours of basketball, but the magic was gone. I'd been on quite a roll earlier in the day, winning lots of my bets and rolling the proceeds over onto the next game. I'd started the day with $100, and my final bet was $1,200 on Arizona . . . who proceeded to lose to Oklahoma. I figured my luck had run its course.

In fact, I'd hit the jackpot.

Chapter 6

AN EPIPHANY

I'd been back in St. Louis for a couple of weeks when I realized that Ed hadn't sent me the book he'd mentioned. I don't know why it popped back into my mind. Maybe it's just that I don't like it when things are left hanging. For whatever reason, I asked Lisa to remind Dorette about Ed's offer to send me the book.

A week or so later, *The Only Guide to a Winning Investment Strategy You'll Ever Need* arrived at my parents' rental house, where I was living in pseudo-exile. The book was a decent-size hardcover, written by a guy named Larry Swedroe.

His name didn't mean anything to me at the time, but I had nothing else to do that morning (after all, I was unemployed). I kicked off my shoes, slumped onto the ratty old futon I used as a couch, and cracked open the book.

Swedroe explained in the book's preface that he was the director of research at Buckingham Asset Management. I thought I knew something about the job of director of research at an investment firm, but the research this guy described was nothing like the research I'd seen at my old firm. Swedroe wasn't in charge of telling his brokers which stocks to buy or sell. He claimed his job was to communicate his firm's investment philosophy to its clients, teach them how to apply it to their own unique circumstances, and keep them up to speed on the latest academic research on how the financial markets behave.

I couldn't quite get my mind around this. He worked for a firm with an investment *philosophy*? His job was to *educate* investors? He kept up on *academic research* on the financial markets?

I kept reading. I finished the preface and started in on the introduction, where the author explained why he'd written the book. He said he wanted to help investors exchange their habits for a more effective investment strategy. He started in on a tennis analogy, which immediately got my attention, because I come from a hard-core tennis family. My grandfather, my parents, my brother, my sister, and I all play, and we're super competitive with each other. We build family vacations around tennis, and our multigenerational commitment to the sport once got us named the US Tennis Association's "Tennis Family of the Year" for the St. Louis area. So when Larry Swedroe started talking about tennis, I was right there with him. Funny as it sounds, the coincidence created a sense that this book held something important for me—that maybe I was meant to be reading it. The feeling was kind of faint at first. But it was about to get stronger.

He said he wanted to help investors exchange their habits for a more effective investment strategy, and I was right there with him. Swedroe's argument went like this: Most tennis players can make an incredible shot once in a while—a pinpoint, practically unhittable delivery deep into an opponent's backhand corner. But trying to win matches that way is a bad idea. The chances of you making those shots again and again are slim. More often, you'll hit the ball long or into the net and end up giving away a point when you go for the amazing shot.[1]

In short, you shouldn't count on your ability to consistently execute those killer shots. Swedroe called that "playing the loser's game." Good tennis players—the ones who make the most of their ability—understand their limits and concentrate on hitting good, safe shots that they know they can consistently execute. They use the center of the court to their advantage, always set themselves up for a return, and wait for their opponents to beat themselves with risky shots. They put the odds in their favor.

What's that got to do with investing? Swedroe asserted that many investors play a losing game with their money by adopting two strategies that reduce their odds of success. First, they try to beat the market by picking individual stocks or other securities, believing that somehow they've spotted a strength or weakness that millions of other investors have overlooked. Second, they try to time exactly when to buy and sell based on the market's outlook, hoping to get in on gains early and then jump out right in time to avoid losses during the next downturn.

Just like a decent tennis player who occasionally makes a killer shot, an investor might sometimes pick a big winner or get out of the stock market just before a big decline in prices. But such bets will fail more often than not, because the odds against winning them are in fact *very* high. And the consequences of losing those risky bets are a lot more serious than losing a match at the local tennis courts.

By this point, I wasn't slumped on the futon casually flipping pages. I was sitting up straight, concentrating on every word. I'd never heard anything like this, and I wanted to know more. Was picking winners on Wall Street or timing market movements really as hard as firing an off-balance backhand down the line on a tennis court?

Swedroe answered my question by laying out the evidence. He clearly had access to tons of academic research related to market returns and investor behavior. No one at my old firm had mentioned any of this stuff during my broker-training program. I felt like I was being let in on a powerful secret.

One of the first studies Swedroe cited analyzed six years' worth of stock trading results for thousands of customers at a large brokerage house. Their attempts at picking winners were dismal failures: The average investor trailed the market's returns by a wide margin. And thanks to the fees and commissions they were paying, the investors who traded the most frequently were the worst off. I immediately thought of Mr. P bullying clients into making trades. How much had their returns suffered?

Another study found that the stocks investors picked actually trailed the market for the 12 months after they bought them. The ones they dumped went on to *beat* the market during the 12 months after the sale. In other words, people were buying high and selling low—the opposite of what successful investors are supposed to do.

It looked like the "loser's game" analogy was spot on. The data showed that investors who followed conventional investing wisdom—pick the stocks you think will beat the market, watch for signs that it's time to buy or sell—were actually only beating themselves. The task was apparently way more difficult—and the odds far worse than most folks realized.

Then again, we were still talking about amateur investors. What about the pros? The financial services industry was built on the idea that their skills could help them beat the market. Almost every week at my brokerage job, I was treated to lunch by mutual fund salesmen from companies touting their portfolio managers' ability to win this game.

I dove back into the book. Reminding me of a courtroom prosecutor, Swedroe went on to lay out the case against *professional* money managers. He cited a study that measured the performance of nearly 2,000 mutual funds over a 30-year period. These funds were run by managers who practiced the standard approach of active management, picking stocks they believed would outperform and trying to time the market's ups and downs. Over the three decades covered by the study, the returns for the average fund in this group significantly trailed its benchmark index, whether it was the S&P 500 or the Russell 2000 or the Dow Jones Industrial Average.

All that work trying to pick stocks and to buy low and sell high was for nothing. Actually, wait. Investors were paying for those efforts in the form of fund management fees, which lowered their returns even further. (And Swedroe hadn't yet mentioned how an active trading strategy adds to investor's tax bills.)

Incredible! I thought to myself. *Wait until everyone has access to this information!* All these highly paid fund managers with their teams of well-compensated analysts and assistants couldn't even match— let alone beat—the market. The experts would have better served their shareholders by not making *any* decisions—just holding all the stocks in their respective areas of concentration, which ranged from small company stocks to giant blue chips to corporate bonds.

But hold on. That study was saying that the *average* fund couldn't beat the market. Why not look for the fund managers who were better than average and give your money to those guys?

It turned out that wouldn't work either.

Sure, most individual investors and fund managers beat their benchmarks on occasion. But it's more or less impossible to find investors or funds that outperform on a consistent basis.

Once again, Swedroe had studies to prove it. Ironically, the most damning evidence showed up in a study published by an investment firm that spent a lot of money trying to convince investors that its active investment approach could consistently outperform the markets. Smith Barney (since absorbed by Citigroup) had studied the performance of 72 stock fund managers over 10 years. During that time, some managers had a few good years, but more often than not, this year's winners were next year's losers.

The book kept piling on the data. How about the gurus who publish investment newsletters? A study of newsletters that tried to pick the best performing mutual funds found that only 10% of them created portfolios that beat the market over a 10-year period. Pathetic. Another study singled out market-timing newsletters—the ones that tell you when to get in and out of stocks. *None* of those guys beat the market over the decade the study covered.

By now, I was feeling a strange mixture of exhaustion and exhilaration. The weight of this information was undeniable: Active management was (and still is) the foundation of Wall Street's business model. I'd been trained to invest this way by a firm with a long history and thousands of brokers and analysts on its payroll. Those people were paid for their supposed skills at picking winning investments. Yet Swedroe was making a convincing case that active management simply doesn't work.

I felt like I'd stumbled on a secret that could change investors' lives while torpedoing Wall Street's current model. No wonder no one at my old firm had ever talked about stuff like this. I'd thought the problem was that my former colleagues weren't trying to help their clients. It's true; they weren't. But this book was saying that my old colleagues couldn't help their clients even if they *wanted* to do so.

Larry Swedroe had dismantled everything I thought I knew about financial markets (which admittedly wasn't much back then), but I wasn't upset. I was starting to get really excited. His book had confirmed my sense that things at my old firm were even worse than I thought. Better yet, he seemed to think there was a better alternative, one grounded in intellectual honesty and rigor.

I felt like I'd stumbled on a secret that could change investors' lives while torpedoing Wall Street's current model.

That alternative was still a little hazy, but in broad terms, it went like this: Instead of trying to outsmart the market and pick individual investments, guys like Swedroe invested in entire categories of stocks or bonds in order to capture the overall growth of global markets around the world without putting too many eggs in any single basket. They used tools similar to index funds, but with a little more science behind them. Then, they held those stakes for the long haul, riding out the market's temporary ups and downs and avoiding all the bad bets and excessive fees that typically eat into investment returns.

Over time, the evidence showed that this approach allowed them to beat the stock pickers and market timers. In effect, it turned the odds in their favor.

I wanted to know more. Meanwhile, I had to check the back cover to confirm that this guy and his firm were really right here in St. Louis. I couldn't believe my luck. Maybe fate was at work.

I read on. The more I read, the more the book made sense to me. I still had questions—such as *why* active management doesn't work and what investors *can* do to achieve superior results over time—but it was enough to understand for the first time that Wall Street's core approach to investing was irreparably flawed.

This fact had two very big implications.

First, it meant that a whole bunch of people had lied to me: the brokers at my first job, the marketers creating ads for big financial institutions, and the media hyping stock picks and superstar fund managers.

The second implication was even more powerful. Not everyone was part of the old, broken model. As I had hoped, some people thought rationally about investing. They were trying to help and even educate investors, not fleece them. They respected their clients' intelligence and worked with them to make smart decisions.

By the time I reached page 100 of Swedroe's 350-page book, I was completely won over. The thoughts racing through my mind crystallized into a single brilliant idea. I jumped up from the futon and grabbed the phone in the kitchen. I was practically shaking as I dialed Lisa's work number. She picked up the phone and said hello, and I made my announcement.

"This is it," I told her. "I know what I want to do for the rest of my life!"

Notes

[1]Larry Swedroe got this tennis analogy from investment advisor Charles Ellis, founder of Greenwich Associates, who wrote about it in 1975. Ellis himself drew on work by scientist and statistician Dr. Simon Ramo, author of *Extraordinary Tennis for the Ordinary Tennis Player*. For more on this, see: https://www.ifa.com/pdfs/ellis_charles_the_losers_game_1975.pdf.

Chapter 7

STORMING THE GATES

Larry Swedroe's evidence was irrefutable. There were the lies that I had witnessed at the first brokerage firm, and there was the truth. The only thing left for me was to join the truth tellers. I had to figure out a way to get a job with Buckingham, where Ed Goldberg and Larry Swedroe worked.

It was thrilling to know what I needed to do, but it also made me a little nervous. I had to call Ed Goldberg, but what if I said the wrong thing and blew my chance to get involved with the work that he and Larry Swedroe were doing? I had no idea whether there were other firms following the same approach, so I felt like this might be my only shot. I had to sell myself to these guys, but how could I make a strong impression? I decided I'd just push through whatever resistance I encountered.

Remember, I was very young. I badly wanted to do something

worthwhile with my life, and so far, I'd been unsuccessful. I didn't even consider what I'd do at Buckingham or whether I could make money there. I thought back to some of my dad's advice: Surround yourself with smart people and learn something valuable. I also figured that if I did work that actually helped people (rather than pretending to help them), I was bound to be successful somehow.

I had no idea at the time just how lucky I was. I had stumbled into the middle of a revolution. The upheaval was in its early stages—still sort of an underground movement—but it was starting to gather momentum.

I would soon learn that Buckingham wasn't alone; it was one of a handful of small firms exploring an investment approach totally unlike the system I'd encountered at my previous job. The new model was based on academic research and historical data about how markets actually behave, rather than on hunches and speculation. The people at Buckingham and their cohorts were also disgusted with the hidden sales agenda of traditional investment firms. They wanted to put clients' interests first by offering sound advice and better investment results—along with lower fees, fewer transaction costs, and better tax management.

I was the perfect candidate to join the emerging evidence-based investing movement. (Back then, we didn't call it that; the phrase "evidence-based" emerged about 15 years later.) The movement's success, even its survival, would depend on its ability to find people crazy or committed enough to think they could take on the Wall

Street establishment. I was young and idealistic and determined to make a difference in the world—and thanks to Larry's book, I was now a true believer.

So on the phone that day, after I announced my discovery, I told Lisa that I was a little freaked out because

I had stumbled into the middle of a revolution. The upheaval was in its early stages, but it was starting to gather momentum.

my entire life plan now depended on getting a job at Ed's firm. She gave me a little pep talk, reminding me that Ed was a nice, normal guy, and that he'd probably be happy to talk with me. So I hung up, took a breath, and dialed Ed Goldberg. I told him I was obsessed with what I'd just read. I told him that his firm's approach seemed to offer what I'd been so desperate to find in the financial services industry. I told him I absolutely *had* to work for his firm because I didn't know of anyone else who was doing anything remotely like what he and his colleagues were doing.

Ed, in his quiet way, tried to talk me down. "Sorry, Matt. We're a small firm, and we don't have any job openings," he said. "We don't even have an HR department."

I kept pressing, insisting that there had to be *someone* at the firm who made hiring decisions. I just needed a chance to come down to the office and make my case. I think Ed was intrigued by my enthusiasm and happy to hear that the light bulb had gone off in my head. I also think he was a little perplexed. He finally said, "Look, you're going to have to call Mont Levy."

Mont isn't your stereotypical HR person—far from it. Forget warm and friendly. Mont is a lawyer by training, and my first phone call with him felt more like an interrogation than an interview. He grilled me about my background and education, and I remember feeling embarrassed because I didn't have the kind of pedigree that I thought would make me stand out. I hadn't attended an Ivy League school or gotten an MBA, and I barely had six months of experience in the financial services industry.

He asked me to describe some of my strengths, and I responded, "I think I'm a reasonably good communicator."

He jumped all over me for that one. "You *think* you're a reasonably good communicator? Well, are you or aren't you?"

I felt like a witness falling apart under cross-examination. "No, I am! I *am* a good communicator," I protested weakly.

After a few more questions, Mont repeated some of Ed's warnings. Buckingham was a small firm. They had no job openings, and even if they did have a spot for me, I'd be taking a big risk signing on with a young firm that might not make it.

I refused to be put off. He finally agreed to let me come into the office to meet him and the team in person.

The next week, I went down to Buckingham's offices, which turned out to be right across the street from my old brokerage firm. I felt a wave of shame as I saw the building where I'd been so confused and disappointed. I didn't want anyone at Buckingham to know that I'd been part of that world. What I didn't know was that several of Buckingham's people had also defected from traditional brokerage firms.

I ducked my head a bit to avoid being recognized by an old colleague, and walked quickly into the lobby of Buckingham's building. I took the elevator to the fourth floor, where I immediately saw that these offices had almost nothing in common with my first workplace. This wasn't an elegant suite decorated in handsome wood and shiny brass. It was just a set of shabby rooms with a bunch of cheap desks jammed together in a space way too small for all of them. Some of those desks even accommodated more than one advisor. In fact, I later learned that the company had grown so fast that they wouldn't have had time to worry about appearances even if they cared.

There was, however, a nice receptionist out front. Donna was warm and friendly. She looked like someone's aunt who probably baked excellent pies. She was expecting me, which was a relief. Donna escorted me through the crowded room to meet Mont, who worked out of a private office just as drab as the main room.

Mont was even more intimidating in person than he'd been on the telephone. Mont isn't tall, but he's physically imposing—a stocky guy with a black beard, dark hair, and a kind of intensity that at first feels sort of threatening. I felt the way I imagined a foot soldier called in front of Napoleon must have felt: The guy was small, but you knew he could crush you. As we shook hands and exchanged greetings, I noticed the pictures on the wall, which featured Mont with world figures: Bill Clinton, Yasser Arafat, even the Pope. *Wait a minute. Who is this guy?* I wondered, feeling a little panicky. *What am I doing here?*

I gathered my wits, reminded myself why I had come, and got ready to press my case. This was the moment that would decide my future. I wasn't leaving until I had some kind of foothold at this company.

We sat around a small side table near Mont's desk. Clinton, Arafat, and the Pope were just over my left shoulder, and it felt like they were looking down at me the whole time. I tried to ignore them and focus on Mont. The first thing he did was to remind me, yet again, that Buckingham had no openings and that even if it did, joining the firm would be a huge risk.

I was getting used to this. I told him none of that mattered to me. I believed strongly in what they were doing, and I wanted to be a part of it at any cost. If they failed, I wanted to fail with them. I told him I didn't care how much they paid me or what they asked me to do. What really got his attention was when I asked this question: "What's one thing you really need help with right now?"

Mont thought it over for a second and mentioned that they had recently started another company called BAM Advisor Services, which helped like-minded advisors run their practices and invest their clients' money. The Advisor Services team could use someone to support new firms in the network. That meant handling billing, account statements, compliance reporting—those sorts of things.

I didn't know exactly what he was talking about, but I said I'd do it. I raised the stakes by promising him I would stay on that job for three years without asking for a promotion. In return, I asked him to make me a promise: After three years, we would talk about my dream of working directly with clients and helping them use their savings to achieve their goals.

For the first time in our conversation, Mont didn't have an immediate counterargument. I think he was impressed by the fact that I just wouldn't give up. I was also willing to sacrifice something to get in the door. This wasn't just a reflection of my determination; it was actually an important consideration for the firm. They needed people who could afford to work for cheap. Buckingham didn't have the budget of a Wall Street giant, so in the early days, they couldn't always pay much. I didn't care. I was young, unmarried, with no kids to support. And I was incredibly hungry to learn what they could teach me.

Mont took me to another office to meet with Bert Schweizer, Buckingham's cofounder. Meeting Bert was like sitting down and talking with someone's kindly and intelligent grandpa. He asked a lot of questions about my background and what made me tick. We talked about why I was so excited by Larry's book, and Bert encouraged my enthusiasm. He said it was warranted; his firm was, in fact, trying to do something special.

After our meeting, Bert walked me back to Mont's office and rendered his verdict with me standing right there: "Hey, I like him," he told Mont. "Bringing him on board sounds good to me."

Mont shrugged his shoulders and grumbled, "Okay. I guess we'll have to figure it out."

And with that, I was hired.

When I finally left the building, I wasn't ducking my head anymore. I was strutting. The folks at Buckingham were trying to change people's lives, and it was hugely gratifying that they felt I could play a role in that.

Looking back, I think they found my enthusiasm encouraging. I wasn't some business school geek who had spent years studying financial market theory, yet after reading 100 pages of Larry Swedroe's book, I understood what they were trying to do.

The fact that I could get so excited so quickly about what they were doing also made it more likely that I'd eventually be of some real use to them. Then again, maybe they weren't all that impressed. Some time later, I asked Mont what finally convinced him to hire me. "You know, Matt," he said. "At the end of the day, I really didn't want to let Dorette Goldberg down."

Chapter 8

JOINING THE MOVEMENT

In August of 1999, I started my job on the BAM Advisor Services side of the business. My duties included helping other advisory firms set up and manage their clients' accounts, coordinating transaction data, processing client billing statements—real nuts-and-bolts stuff. But while I wasn't in the room with advisors and their clients, I was immersed in the evidence-based investing movement from the day I walked in.

Everyone in the company was as excited about this investing approach as I was. They couldn't help talking about it—sharing new ideas, asking questions, and debating the answers. It was unbelievable. No one at my first job ever shared ideas, for fear of losing ground on the daily production blotter. And no one talked about investing philosophy because they didn't have one. In this new world, everyone wanted to understand how the financial markets worked so they could help their clients.

They also wanted everyone in the company to play a role in that mission. My colleagues became my mentors, explaining what they believed, why they believed it, and how they translated those beliefs into investment portfolios for their clients. These ongoing discussions helped me understand more fully *why* the traditional investing approach of picking stocks and trying to time the markets didn't work.

I quickly discovered that the foundation of the evidence-based investing movement was an idea known as the efficient market hypothesis (EMH), which was formulated in the 1960s by Eugene Fama,[1] a professor at the University of Chicago Booth School of Business, who was studying how markets price assets.

Fama's conclusion, which gave the hypothesis its name, was that financial markets are very efficient at processing information. That means that when some news or data comes out that might affect the value of a company's stock or bonds, the market quickly incorporates it into the price of those assets.

In this new world, everyone wanted to understand how the financial markets worked so they could help their clients.

Let's say a company announces several new, long-term contracts that are likely to boost revenues and profits for years to come. Or, imagine a major earthquake destroys the factory that provides the key component of the firm's flagship product. Either event could have big implications for the future value of that company's stock. The EMH maintains that the market itself (meaning the sum of all the millions of institutional and individual investors out there) quickly absorbs and responds to that information. As a result, the stock's price immediately rises or falls to reflect the market's collective take on its current value.

The upshot is that—for all practical purposes—the price of a stock or bond reflects all of the public information available to investors at any given time. This means it's virtually impossible to find a truly overvalued or undervalued investment. In other words, the Holy Grail of the traditional approach to investing—the undervalued investment—is essentially a myth.

Take, for instance, our hypothetical company again. An investor reading the news about its new contracts might make the reasonable assumption that revenues will grow and the stock price will rise, and might buy the stock in the belief that the firm's improved outlook will drive the price higher. The trouble is that millions of other investors have also heard the news, made the same assumption, and bought the stock. As a result, the value of those future contracts is already reflected in the stock price.

The efficient market hypothesis made sense to me. And it fit the facts. It explained why most investors failed to beat the market over time. It explained the results of all those studies I'd read about in Larry Swedroe's book.

Investors out there who thought they knew something the rest of the market didn't know were wrong. The market knew what they knew. You couldn't expect to beat the market by acting on publicly available information. (Inside information, maybe, but that's illegal.)

Since Fama came up with the efficient market hypothesis, more than 40 years ago, academics have proposed many variations on the theory. Moreover, people who basically believe the theory still debate just how efficient the markets really are. But as my colleagues at Buckingham explained, it doesn't matter whether the markets are 100% efficient. The most important implication of the efficient market hypothesis is that the markets are efficient enough that it's extremely difficult, and maybe impossible, for any investor to out-smart them consistently.

We can concede that markets aren't *perfectly* efficient. Once in a great while, you might actually spot an investment that's underval-ued or overvalued and make your move before the rest of the market catches on. But it's highly unlikely that any given investor can consistently exploit those inefficiencies. Given that, active investing is basically a form of gambling.

Investors who try to outguess the market's verdict on an asset typically get it wrong more often than they get it right. As a result, their losses, especially when combined with the cost of the hunt (taxes and fees), will outweigh whatever gains they achieve.

The evidence-based investing community had decided that it

wasn't worth betting a client's life savings on the very slim chance that we, or any investment manager, could consistently outwit the collective wisdom of the market. Instead, we accepted that efficiency was an inherent part of the market, and we designed our investing strategy to reflect that reality.

Active investing is basically a form of gambling.

The notion that the markets are efficient was universal at the firm. Everyone got it—even new guys like me—and it informed almost every decision we made. Our success putting that data and evidence to work for clients reinforced everyone's conviction that the market's inherent efficiency changed the entire investing game. After a while, the efficient market hypothesis kind of sank into your DNA.

Looking back, I see that we were a lot like the statistics geeks who were starting to infiltrate the equally traditional world of baseball around the same time—a movement famously described by Michael Lewis in his book *Moneyball.* The *Moneyball* geeks were passionate about using data, evidence, and statistical analysis to build better baseball teams. We were passionate about using data to build better investment portfolios. The *Moneyball* approach was in direct conflict with the traditional ways of managers, coaches, and scouts who, for decades, had relied on a system of subjective assessments, gut instinct, and just plain guesses to rate players. Similarly, we were flying in the face of old-school investment managers, who picked stocks because they liked the company's product or believed they had some crucial but overlooked piece of information that the rest of the market had missed.

We felt like I imagine the *Moneyball* geeks felt when their movement was coming of age: totally confident that we were right and the traditionalists were wrong. The data and evidence just made too much sense to ignore.

Like the *Moneyball* guys, we also felt completely outnumbered. We had begun to establish a beachhead in the investing world, but it didn't yet amount to much. Inside the walls of our shabby, cluttered office, we were all true believers. But when we ventured outside to talk with potential clients, we encountered people who weren't enthusiastic about our ideas.

Our challenge was to convince those unbelievers to join the revolution. And as I was about to discover, it wouldn't be easy.

Notes

[1] Eugene F. Fama, "Efficient Capital Markets: A Review of Theory and Empirical Work," *The Journal of Finance* 25, no. 2 (May, 1970): 383–417.

Chapter 9

SIDEKICK

From the moment I started my new job, I couldn't wait to meet Larry Swedroe, whose book had rocked my world. He worked from home and didn't come into the office very often, but I heard he'd be attending a daylong retreat the firm held at a local hotel during my first week on the job. I was actually going to be in a room with my new hero. I wanted to express my gratitude to the man, but I was nervous. How should I approach him? What should I say?

The retreat started early in the morning, so there was no time to seek him out before things got going. I didn't see Larry at the first two sessions. After the second one broke up, I walked down the hall to the men's room. I pushed open the door, and there he was: Larry Swedroe.

It was obviously Larry. Apart from the circumstances, he looked like he did in his book photo. I couldn't believe it. This was far from the ideal place for a conversation—but I had to stand there and wait my turn anyway, and who knew when I'd have another chance to talk to him? When he turned and walked toward the sink to wash his hands, I spoke up. My first words to the man: "Are you Larry?" (Even though I knew he was.)

He was dressed casually, in a polo shirt and khakis. And while he wasn't quite as tall as I'd expected, he was clearly very fit. He seemed puzzled, which made sense; some stranger was talking to him in the bathroom. He said, "Yes, I'm Larry."

As he began washing his hands I took the opportunity to introduce myself. I said I was the firm's newest employee and that this was my first week on the job. Then, I gave what I thought was a heartfelt little speech: "I want to let you know that I read your book, and it's the reason I'm here. It totally inspired me to pursue this career, and I can't thank you enough."

He shook the water off his hands and headed for the towels. Then, he looked at me dismissively and said. "Nice try, Mike. Kissing up to the partner during your first week. Not. Gonna. Work."

And with that, he walked out of the bathroom, leaving me stunned. *He thought I was a kiss-ass? He thought my name was Mike? How had things gone so wrong, so quickly?*

I needn't have worried. This was classic Larry—nothing to take personally. Larry is a son of the Bronx and still retains much of his tough New York accent and attitude. He's also ridiculously smart and driven. He graduated from college at 19 and earned his MBA

at 21. By age 25, he was running foreign exchange and risk management departments at global financial institutions. As a kid responsible for millions of dollars, overseeing people twice his age, he had
to be tough—and he never entirely lost the habit.

Another thing about Larry: He isn't content to preach to the
choir. He seeks out people who are likely to resist his ideas, so he can
try to convince them that an evidence-based investment approach
works. He loves the challenge, and he feels like this sparring keeps
him sharp. And when he has the facts on his side, he's not afraid to
be loud. His version of mentoring is kind of like hitting you over
the head until you comply with his take on things—the truth, in
other words.

As I pondered my first, supremely awkward exchange with Larry,
I made a decision: I wouldn't let anything discourage me from
learning whatever I could from him. As it turned out, Larry didn't
hold his first impression against me, either. In fact, he soon started
seeking me out for short conversations. He would often walk up
to my desk and yell (it always seemed like he was yelling), "Mike,
how's it going?" He called me Mike for my first three months on
the job. "What kinds of questions are advisors asking you lately?"

Other times, he'd drop off a copy of something he'd just written,
like a presentation to investors or even a chapter of a new book, and
ask for my thoughts on it. (Larry did this with a lot of folks in the
office; he liked to get feedback on his work.) I would always read
what he gave me, and he would always come back to hear what I

thought. Of course, Larry being Larry, he'd usually listen to my feedback and then tell me why I was wrong. But it was all part of the learning experience.

Eventually, I became something of a sidekick to him. Part of my job on the advisor services side was helping the firms in our network grow their practices, and one of our best marketing tactics was sending Larry out to speak to advisor clients and prospects. I was in charge of scheduling these talks for Larry, and I ended up driving him to the ones that took place within three or four hours of St. Louis.

Because I was with him anyway, it naturally fell to me to be his on-site assistant. When we arrived at a venue where Larry was giving a talk, I'd lug in a box of his books for him to sign, then set up his computer and an easel with a large pad of paper, which he liked to use during his presentation. While Larry spoke, I would sit off to the side and click the button to advance his slides (Larry hated using the handheld clicker while he was talking). It was pretty menial stuff. Another ambitious kid might have taken the assignment as an insult. Me? I felt like I was on a roll.

The gig gave me hours and hours of uninterrupted time in the car with Larry—time I could use to pick his brain on how the markets worked, how to help clients, and how to handle the inevitable questions and objections that we faced from investors. Meanwhile, I had a front-row seat for the Larry show, so I could watch him give his audiences a dose of the potentially life-changing information I'd first encountered in his book.

I loved feeling like I was helping to bring the evidence-based revolution to investors all over the Midwest. And I could tell that Larry liked these trips as much as I did, which was kind of surprising. Here was a guy who had held important positions at big banks, and who was now partner and research director at a growing investment advisory firm. I figured he had more important things to do, but he was totally game to drive three hours in the dead of winter to speak to tiny gatherings of people in places like Peoria, Illinois, or Cape Girardeau, Missouri.

> *I loved feeling like I was helping to bring the evidence-based revolution to investors all over the Midwest.*

When I asked him why he bothered, he told me about a physician he'd met at a recent conference. This doctor made a good living, and like a lot of smart, successful people, he thought he could turn his excess cash into serious wealth by investing in the stock market. He started reading investing books and newsletters. Pretty soon, he was obsessively checking stock charts and reading the financial news. He'd come home from work and take his dinner into his study so he could check his daily returns and plan his next moves. He ended up paying more attention to his portfolio than to his family. His marriage collapsed.

Shortly after that, someone gave the doctor a copy of Larry's book. At first, the doctor tried to poke holes in Larry's logic. But when he looked back at his own stock trading record, he saw that in spite of his brains and hard work, he had made a lot more bad bets than good ones. He'd damaged his marriage and his relationship with his daughter trying to beat the market, and he hadn't even kept pace with the market's overall returns. He told Larry that if he'd read the book 10 years earlier, his life would have been completely different.

Larry wasn't out there to sell more books or get famous. He had no interest in how much money his books would make for him. (He had made lots of money already, and had invested it successfully.) He wasn't out on the road for personal gain. He was out there to change lives.

Chapter 10

THE BIG ROCKS

Larry and I felt like we were on a lofty mission (I wanted to change lives too!), but we pursued it by humble means. Whenever Larry had a speaking gig, I'd go rent a car—usually a boring, mid-sized sedan. We'd leave for our appointments early enough to arrive at the venue two hours before the start of Larry's talk. He didn't want traffic or bad weather to make us late, and getting there early gave him more time to meet clients, answer advisors' questions, and sign books.

When we got in the car, we typically had a long drive ahead of us. Larry would immediately say something like this: "Matt, I really shouldn't talk much. I have to save my voice for tonight's presentation."

Then, he'd talk nonstop for the next two hours.

He spent a lot of that time criticizing my driving—telling me I didn't know how to merge, reminding me to use my blinkers, that sort of thing. We also talked about our families and tennis (like me, he's a passionate tennis player, which explained the tennis metaphor he used early in his book). We started getting to know each other as people.

I also made a point of asking Larry questions about the markets and how to create a winning investment strategy. Early in our relationship, he talked about the Lake Wobegon effect, named for Garrison Keillor's fictional town, where "all the children are above average." Larry maintained that investors held a similar delusion about themselves—they all thought they were going to beat the market—and Wall Street was in no hurry to disillusion them. That was our job.

Looking back, I like to cast myself as a young Jonah Hill following Brad Pitt around the Midwest, spreading the revolution to Middle America in our version of the *Moneyball* story. But there was nothing Hollywood about our situation. This really *was* Middle America, in all its everyday, ordinary glory. Sometimes Larry gave his talks in hotel meeting rooms or restaurants, but more often than not, we were booked in school gyms or auditoriums, which were the biggest rooms available in some of these small towns. On a typical night, there would be 50 or so people in the audience—mostly older, affluent types, the kind of clients who tend to attract the interest of financial advisors.

But I tell you what: These folks had never seen anything like the presentation Larry was about to give them. For starters, Larry's rough-around-the-edges style contrasted sharply with the slick ways of the salesmen that Wall Street firms send out to recruit new clients. Larry came off like a tough New Yorker. He talked a mile a minute to these nice midwestern folks. He also committed every PowerPoint sin in the book. His slides were so dense with text that you could barely read the tiny words projected on the screen. When he did add graphics, they were often charts that baffled anyone who wasn't a math geek. He also had way too many slides. Inevitably, he'd fall behind schedule, and then race through the end of his presentation, which meant he talked even faster.

The content of the talk was even more jarring than the presentation. Larry would start out the way he began his book, explaining that traditional active investing was like playing the loser's game in tennis. Then he'd begin hammering away at the evidence he'd collected to show that active investors simply can't beat the market consistently.

He had one chart showing that during the previous decade, barely 10% of the top-25 performing mutual funds from any given year were able to repeat their top-25 performance the following year. He'd show the chart and point out that if you tried to hop on the bandwagon of a hot fund on the basis of the previous year's performance, you would, as a rule, be sorely disappointed.

A study of the performance of 30 of the biggest pension fund managers—ostensibly some of the world's smartest and most experienced investors—found that only four were able to beat a simple index-fund portfolio of 60% stocks and 40% bonds.

Another study that looked at 13 years' worth of returns for the S&P 500 showed how damaging it could be to try to time the market: If investors missed just the 10 best days of the stock market's performance during the 13-year period, their returns would be 30% lower than what they could have earned by simply buying and holding stocks. If they missed the 30 best trading days, either by sitting on the sidelines and waiting for the right time to get in, or by selling too soon, their returns would have been more than 60% lower than what they'd have earned using a buy-and-hold strategy.

It was a pile-on, like his book. And while Larry didn't demonize Wall Street or flat-out call them crooks, he made sure the audience understood that the fees and commissions their current brokers charged were further undermining their investment returns.

Watching all this from the front of the room, I could see that most people weren't nearly as open to Larry's message as I had been. The tension in the audience was evident. People sat with their arms folded, leaning back and fidgeting in their seats. The first time I saw this, I started to think about Larry's message from their point of view: This abrasive guy was saying that everything you thought you knew about investing was wrong. It was as if he was calling them out as dupes of a flawed system, or as active participants in an investment strategy that was actually working against them.

Larry knew his message was a hard one to hear, but he didn't mind being the one who had to deliver it. People were losing money every day and failing to achieve their goals because they had a warped—or at least inaccurate—picture of reality. They needed to know the truth.

Eventually, someone in the audience would stand up during the Q&A portion of the presentation and say something along these lines: "Well, that might be true for some people, but not for me. My broker is different."

Larry would take that as his cue to bring up the Lake Wobegon effect: "Of course you think you and your broker are above-average investors. Everyone else In this room believes that they and their broker are also above-average investors. That doesn't make it true, does it?" Then he'd ask the members of the audience to raise their hands if they thought they were above-average drivers. When three-quarters of the room put their hands up, he'd proved his point.

> *People were losing money every day and failing to achieve their goals because they had a warped—or at least inaccurate—picture of reality. They needed to know the truth.*

Still, I could see how Larry's critique of a traditional, active investment approach seemed almost, well . . . *un-American*. The American dream is the idea that you can get ahead if you're smart and willing to work harder than everyone else. We were telling people that no matter how smart they were or how hard they worked, they had little chance of getting better-than-average returns from a traditional active investing approach—and almost no chance of doing it year after year.

The primary explanation for this, of course, was the efficient market hypothesis. Larry would diligently explain that it is difficult to find truly undervalued or overvalued investments, chiefly because the markets are so good at incorporating relevant information into the price of an asset. In other words, he'd tell these folks, you don't know anything the market doesn't already know.

Larry would then immediately wade further into the theory, exploring some of the technical details behind it. That's when I could sense people going numb. Some would squint at Larry's terrible slides; others just looked dumbfounded. They had come to the event expecting wine and cheese and a sales pitch. Instead, they found themselves in a graduate school seminar on finance.

It wasn't just the data overload. People were also taken aback by the implications of what Larry was saying. He had systematically demolished the common belief that investment success comes from picking stocks and trying to predict where the market is going. A lot of the folks in our audience were wondering what in the world they were supposed to do if we were right. Should they just give up and stop investing?

Not at all. Larry would explain that there is a better way to invest—one based on data and evidence about how the markets really work. That evidence shows us that predictions and guesses are worthless. But while that might feel unsettling at first, a whole world of new possibilities opens up once you embrace the fact that the markets are efficient.

Rather than trying to pick winners and time the market's ups and downs, you can harness the growth of the global economy. You do that by investing in funds similar to index funds that target different areas of the market (and their expected returns)—small company stocks, large company stocks, international stocks, and so on. The right mix of such funds depends on your unique circumstances, but once you make a plan, you *stick with it*, letting the financial markets do their job.

When you do this, you significantly improve your odds of success by avoiding losses on bad bets. You also avoid the classic market-timing mistake of buying high and selling low. You don't get whipsawed trying to keep pace with the fluctuating fortunes of a particular investment or short-term changes in market conditions. And by turning down the volume on your investing activity, you reduce the brokerage fees and taxes that accompany every useless transaction.

> *He had systematically demolished the common belief that investment success comes from picking stocks and trying to predict where the market is going.*

I found the data and evidence behind the efficient market hypothesis pretty compelling. I was Larry's acolyte, after all. But as

I watched those audiences a couple of times a month, I realized that something else about our investment philosophy tended to resonate with them a lot more. It came at the end of Larry's presentation, after he'd been beating them over the head for an hour with academic studies. To wrap up his talk, he would bring the discussion down to the personal level by telling his "big rocks" story. It goes like this:

One day, a professor was speaking to her class of business school students about the importance of time management. She placed a large glass jar on her desk and filled it with fist-sized rocks, one by one, until she couldn't fit any more inside. Then, she asked the class, "Is this jar full?"

Most of the class replied "Yes." She then took out a bag of gravel and dropped handfuls of it into the jar, where the gravel slid into the spaces between the big rocks. "Now is it full?" she asked. These were smart kids, and they'd caught on by then, so a few ventured that it probably wasn't full.

"Well, let's see," said the professor, as she took out a bucket of sand and dumped it into the jar. With a few shakes, the sand filled in the gaps around the gravel. "Now, is it full?" she asked. Although the class wasn't sure what was smaller than sand, they figured she had something planned, so they all called out, "No!"

Sure enough, the professor took out a jug of water and poured it into the jar, where it took up all the space around the rocks, sand, and gravel, filling the jar to the brim. She then explained the point of her demonstration: If you don't put the big rocks in first, you'll never get them in around all that other little stuff.

Busy people's lives are like that jar. They can always find ways to squeeze more and more little things into their lives—more meetings, more commitments, more distractions. But if they don't take care of their big rocks first, they'll never have room for them. Most people's "big rocks" are things like family, friends, community, education, career, hobbies: the things that really bring joy and satisfaction. The professor urged her students to put them first.

Larry urged his audiences to think of this message in the context of their investing strategy. People who follow a traditional, active management approach tend to spend way too much time reading investment news, researching different investment options, chasing the next hot stock or fund manager, and worrying about short-term market swings. They spend too much time buying and selling investments, tinkering with their portfolio in hopes that it will deliver higher returns. Apart from being useless, those activities are all gravel, sand, and water. They distract us from the big rocks: the things that we save and invest for in the first place.

People who embrace evidence-based investing can skip the distractions. Instead, they can choose a mix of investments based on the best evidence about how markets perform over time and then hold on to those investments for the long term. They can tune out the noise from the investing world and focus on living their lives. As a result, they will probably achieve better investment returns, *and* they will improve their odds of finding happiness.

Every time Larry told this story, I could feel the vibe in the room shift. People's body language changed. They leaned forward in their seats. What grabbed these folks was not so much the logic and science behind our approach but the freedom that this type of investing could offer. The science suddenly felt relevant.

That part of the evening usually felt pretty good. But then Larry would stop talking and open the floor for questions. I don't want to say all hell would break loose—but the good vibes tended to vanish.

Chapter 11

WHAT ABOUT WARREN BUFFETT?

The first question for Larry almost always came from someone eager to challenge his evidence and defend the cause of active management. Typically, the questioner was an overconfident male with a big ego—maybe a broker from a competing firm or someone related to a broker—who felt threatened by every word that came out of Larry's mouth. It's hard for the pros to admit that their picks and prognostications are useless, because if they do, they're essentially out of a job. We've all heard of fight-or-flight syndrome. These guys wanted to fight.

I remember one night noticing a slightly pudgy, middle-aged guy in a suit. He was sitting in an aisle seat, probably so he could sneak out unnoticed if the talk was boring. But Larry didn't bore him. The guy was soon sitting on the edge of his chair, tapping his foot impatiently. He tossed in a few headshakes and grimaces at some of

Larry's data points. After a while, I realized that this guy wasn't just skeptical; he was pissed off.

Larry finished on his usual uplifting note about focusing on the important things in life and asked the crowd for questions. Sure enough, this guy shot up a hand. He could barely keep himself in his seat. It was clear he wanted to destroy Larry's argument and humiliate him.

Larry called on the purple-faced time bomb, who visibly gathered himself before beginning to speak. His tone was patronizing, almost mocking. He said something along the lines of, "Well, Mr. Swedroe, this is a very interesting *theory*, but I'm not sure you academics understand how the real world works. How would you explain people like me who have been very successful in life and are doing just fine with our investing strategy?"

Larry knew better than to fight emotion with emotion. He waited patiently for the guy to finish his question and calmly responded. "Thank you for your question. I'm glad to hear you've had some success, but let me show you something that might put this performance into perspective."

With that, he launched into another of his favorite lessons: The coin-flip experiment. He invited a woman from the front row to stand up and imagine that she had to flip a coin 50 times. Then, he handed her a pen and told her to walk over to the easel and write down the sequence of heads and tails generated from these imaginary coin tosses. The woman wrote down a series of Hs and Ts in her approximation of a random pattern—mostly alternating heads and tails, but sometimes repeating two heads in a row, then later a few tails in a row, and so on.

Larry thanked her then told her that she (like most people) had greatly underestimated the potential for streaks of heads and tails. Statistics tell us that if she had tossed a real coin, we could easily have seen five, six, seven, even 13 heads in a row. Larry acknowledged that it's hard for us to imagine that such patterns can really be random, yet each coin flip has the same odds of showing heads or tails no matter what happened the time before. Over the full sequence of 50 flips, we expect to see a roughly even distribution of heads and tails, but there's no law saying that we get there in a nice, even pattern. A few long streaks of both heads and tails are perfectly within the realm of probability.

How did this weird statistics lesson apply to investing? Larry got to the point: Everyone knows there's nothing a coin flipper can do to actually increase his chances of getting heads or tails consistently. Those long streaks are pure chance. But when similar patterns occur in the market—a hot mutual fund manager beats the market for a few years in a row—we're quick to attribute them to the investor's skill. This is a costly mistake, given the mountain of academic studies showing that such results are almost exclusively a matter of luck.

It all added up to an uncomfortable truth for guys like our purple-faced friend, who thought Larry's talk had no bearing on the real world of investing. As Larry put it, "It's nice you've had some success with your investments recently, but the odds of that success continuing are not good."

At this point, someone would jump up to challenge Larry with the name of a famous, successful investor. Most of the time it was, "What about Warren Buffett? He beats the market all the time!"

Larry's answer was always the same, whether the example was Buffett or someone like Peter Lynch, who steered Fidelity's Magellan Fund to spectacular gains during his 13-year tenure. First, he'd acknowledge that you can't just ignore a track record like Buffett's. But if that record is really based on skill, shouldn't Buffett or Lynch be able to teach that skill to others who can repeat his success? Why is there only one Warren Buffett? Why aren't there more superstar fund managers like Peter Lynch? There are more than 2,000 mutual fund managers out there trying to make a name for themselves by outsmarting the market, yet how many of these managers have become household names?

What's more, Larry continued, we can only recognize Buffett's genius or Lynch's amazing track record after the fact. You simply can't know whether the fund manager you think is the next Peter Lynch will really win in the long term. And as we've seen, for every Buffett, there are countless other investors who have failed to beat the market over 20 or 30 years.

Finally, Larry would ask the audience three questions: "Are you willing to bet your life savings that you can pick the next Buffett or Lynch? Can you be that confident in your choice? Isn't it more likely that you'll end up jumping from fund to fund over the next 10 or 15 years—hurting your returns and racking up taxes and transaction costs along the way?"

Sometimes, people took other angles of attack. The efficient market hypothesis seems to posit a rational market that values stocks and other assets on the basis of all the known facts. But we were traveling around in 1999 and 2000, at the height of the Internet bubble. Not surprisingly, people often asked questions along these lines: "If the markets are really efficient, how can you explain this Internet craze that's going on right now? When a stock opens at $30 and goes up to $100 in one day, I can triple my money How Is that efficient? Meanwhile, you're telling me I should buy index funds! That makes no sense!"

This one didn't throw Larry either. First, he'd calmly remind the audience that he never said the markets are *perfectly* efficient. Efficiency is a framework we use to understand how markets work. Within this framework, we know there can be weird anomalies and short-term inefficiencies that are difficult to explain. After all, Larry would remind people, markets are made up of human beings, and humans often behave in unpredictable ways. Then he'd urge people to ask themselves this question: Do you really think you're the person who can find and exploit such inefficiencies over and over again? Bubbles have obviously happened in the past and will continue to happen. But for active investors to consistently make money on bubbles, they need to invest in the right things at the right time *and* get out with their gains before the bubble bursts. That's not easy to do.

In short, Larry's argument was that the chances of anyone out-smarting the market are extremely low. He'd urge people not to bet their life savings and their future financial security on the idea that they were the rare exception to the rule. Instead, they could take a look at the evidence and then choose an investment strategy that puts the odds on their side.

There was one other question we heard from almost every audience we met. This one gave us the most hope for the success of our revolution, because it showed that we'd gotten people to think critically about the traditional, active investing approach. Each night, someone would ask a variation on this theme: "If what you're saying is true, how come everyone isn't investing this way?"

It's a question we continue to ponder. One reason is that a lot of people simply don't know that this evidence-based investing approach exists. Most people start out with almost no preconceived notions about how to invest their money. Investing and finance isn't part of the basic high school or college curriculum, and most of us don't think much about investing until we're earning a salary and starting to consider long-term goals like buying a home, launching a business, putting kids through

Take a look at the evidence and then choose an investment strategy that puts the odds on your side.

college, and saving for retirement. That's when we get caught up by powerful forces that perpetuate the fantasy of the traditional investing model.

Meanwhile, we're confronted by the two-headed monster of Wall Street's marketing machine and the financial media. Both heads spout the same message: To be financially successful, you have to beat the market. And the only way to beat the market is by picking the right investments and knowing precisely the right time to buy and sell them.

Wall Street spends billions of dollars to get that message out there in the form of paid advertisements. Worse, the media often touts the same story. They need you to keep reading, clicking, watching, or listening, so they keep pumping out new investment recommendations and market predictions. They also need to keep their advertisers happy. It's not good business to discredit the results of the investment firms and mutual funds they rely on for the bulk of their revenues. There are some stories about the evidence-based investing model (way more today than back in the 1990s), but that coverage is still overshadowed by headlines about this year's hot stocks.

Such forces have created a common narrative about investing that people can't help internalizing. But as Larry told his audiences, they were the lucky ones: They had now seen the evidence. They could stay with the old model and continue to pay excessive fees for poor performance, or they could invest in line with the evidence and greatly increase their odds of achieving long-term success and peace of mind.

Typically, a few people got it. They'd come up to us after the talk and say how refreshing it was to hear something so unlike the typical Wall Street marketing pitch. I could see the wheels turning in their minds. They were starting to see the world differently.

It was a start. Still, in those early days, I was confused and a little frustrated. Why didn't more people get this? After a while, I realized that it wasn't just Wall Street that was in love with its broken model. Investors themselves had a hard time letting go of the idea that they could win by picking the right investments or betting on the hottest fund managers. Our task felt a lot like trying to get people to exercise more or eat healthier. Despite mountains of data, most people simply refused to change their habits.

We couldn't stop some people from gambling with their savings. But who was I to judge them? Betting is fun! Big wins are exciting! I was probably the most zealous recruit in the history of this movement, and I still had some problems cutting my ties to the old investing model. Back when I worked at my first brokerage firm, I'd bought shares of some hot technology stocks. After reading Larry's book, I stopped trying to pick winners, but I hung on to my old Qualcomm and Amazon.com shares. I saw them as lottery tickets, and I still hoped I might win the jackpot.

They were still in my portfolio when I joined Buckingham and transferred my investments to an account with the firm. My account statement showed up on the daily report reconciling all our clients' account activity—and guess who noticed my little technology stake? One morning right after our accounts system issued its daily status report, Larry came stomping over to me from across the room. He didn't say hello. His greeting was "Mike. I thought you read my book."

I was confused. I stammered that of course I'd read it. I'd *loved* it! Then, Larry held up a piece of paper he'd been carrying and said, "I don't think so! I just saw the report of new accounts that were transferred to us. You're holding Amazon and Qualcomm? You're not even invested in the funds we recommend. What's your problem?"

I had no real excuse. I had set up my new 401(k) to invest in all the funds the firm recommended, but I couldn't bring myself to sell these shares yet. I told Larry I'd sell them right away and reinvest the money according to our plan. When I unloaded them that day, I lost about $2,000. Larry said to think of it as tuition: I'd just paid a very reasonable fee for a lesson that would almost certainly pay huge dividends over the remaining decades of my life.

I had also learned another lesson: It's incredibly hard to leave the old investing world behind. I was starting to see that even the best data sometimes isn't enough to change people's habits. We needed to change people's hearts as well as their minds.

Chapter 12

THE ISLAND OF IDEALISM

While Larry was teaching me the science behind our investment strategy, another mentor was helping me understand the human side of the investing business. His name was Rick Hill. Meeting Rick set in motion another series of changes that altered the course of my career and my life.

The meeting occurred on my second day at Buckingham. Donna, the friendly receptionist, was giving me an official tour of our offices. Buckingham had originally occupied a small suite, but the firm had taken over half a floor as it grew. Now, a string of rooms ran down one side of the building and doglegged around a corner.

My tour ended abruptly at four cubicles crammed into a space that would have felt small even for one person. Sitting at one of the cubicles was a fellow who looked like he belonged in better accommodations. He had white hair that was neatly cut, and he peered at me through a pair of tortoiseshell glasses. He wore khaki pants and a plaid shirt. He looked vaguely distinguished. You could easily imagine him sitting in a fancy corner office or at a conference table in a corporate boardroom, but he seemed completely relaxed. His crummy workspace clearly didn't bother him. I was intrigued, so I made a mental note to return for a visit.

I did just that when lunchtime rolled around a couple of hours later. The white-haired guy was still at his desk, so I introduced myself and started asking questions. It's a habit I've had since childhood. When I meet new people, I try to learn as much as I can about them. Sometimes, my approach can be a little jarring.

"Hi. I'm Matt Hall," I said. "Who are you?"

"I'm Rick Hill."

"What are you doing here?"

"I'm working."

"No, I mean what are you doing here at Buckingham. What's your story?"

He paused, a little confused, then started to explain how he'd come to Buckingham after working at Anheuser-Busch. I interrupted him to clarify my question: I wanted his whole story, starting with where he was born.

"Delaware," he said.

"I don't know anyone from there," I said. "What's it like?"

By now, he was looking at me like he couldn't decide if I was kind of interesting or just annoying. He then sketched out his biography for me. I learned that he'd earned his undergraduate degree at Wake Forest University, had gone to Wharton for business school, had worked as stockbroker in the late '60s and early '70s, and had then joined the finance department at Anheuser-Busch. He had eventually become the company's assistant treasurer. Between the corporate title and the Wharton degree, I was even more confused by the fact that he was stuck at the end of a hallway at Buckingham—and completely at ease with the situation.

I asked him if he had plans for lunch. He told me he usually just grabbed a sandwich by himself and found a quiet place to read *The Wall Street Journal*. "Not anymore," I told him. "Starting today, you and I are having lunch together."

Rick was taken aback by my assumption that he'd want to have lunch with me even once, let alone multiple times. But for whatever reason, he agreed to join me. Maybe, like Mont Levy, he sensed that I just would not give up. I also think he was a little curious about me. It's not every day that a 20-something shows up wanting to know everything about you and your life.

We headed for the restaurant on the ground floor of our office building. I decided I wanted to figure out how Rick's long career had brought him to the place where mine was just beginning. We found a table, and I asked him about his experience as a stockbroker when he was my age. The story was frighteningly similar to mine, even though it had taken place 30 years earlier.

Rick, as a newly minted MBA back then, was more interested

in finance than business management. So he took a job as a broker, expecting to learn how to put the financial markets to work for his clients. Instead, the only training he got was in selling—how to cold call, how to put the hard sell on waffling clients, that sort of thing. When it came time to actually pick investments for his clients, he realized he had a problem. He didn't know which stocks would do better or worse than others. In fact, he sensed that traditional stock picking was basically a form of gambling, and he felt awful about gambling with his clients' money.

His unease deepened when the firm started pressuring him to bring in his friends and family as clients. He sold them stocks and then felt terrible that he couldn't control the outcomes. He was embarrassed that he had no good explanation for their losses. He grew so ashamed that when he'd drive home to visit his parents, he'd ask them to move a car out of the garage so he could park inside. He didn't want any of his old friends and neighbors to see his car and know he was home. He couldn't face them.

I told him I completely understood the feeling. I would have been hiding from my friends and family if I had stayed at my first brokerage firm job much longer. Rick had gone on trying his best, making recommendations that he hoped would benefit his clients, yet always feeling like the whole system was stacked against the people it was supposed to serve.

He began noticing a game the other brokers in his office often played. When one broker was on the phone, talking to clients about making a potential trade, the others would stand around waiting for a signal. If the client was a buyer, the broker on the phone would signal a thumbs-up and then ask loudly what the people in the room thought about Stock X. The guys standing around would hoot and holler false encouragement about what a great buy it was. If the client was a seller, the broker on the phone would give a thumbs-down before he asked about the stock, and the crowd would boo and shout things like "No way! It's a dog!" It was pure theater. No one really knew or cared about the stock's potential. They were just trying to urge the client to make the trade, because trades equaled commissions.

Rick decided he couldn't live the lie anymore, and he quit. He contacted the Wharton career office and discovered a job opening at Anheuser-Busch in the corporate finance department. It sounded better than gambling with people's savings, so he came to St. Louis thinking he'd left the world of investing for good.

Twenty years passed. Around the beginning of the 1990s, Anheuser-Busch executives took a hard look at the cost of running the company's multibillion-dollar pension and retirement plans—especially the fees they were paying to professional advisors. The firm had picked these advisors on the basis of past performance, but few had been able to generate returns that consistently beat the market.

The company's pension committee was tired of overpaying for underperformance, so it made a radical move: It switched the entire pension plan into an index-based strategy. They would simply invest pension funds in vehicles that mirrored the makeup of broad market indexes. No more picking stocks and trying to time the market; they'd capture whatever gains or losses the market delivered each year while saving tons of money in fees.

Few companies had even seen the evidence against active investing back then, and even fewer had taken a stand like this one. As a member of the finance department, Rick saw the data that convinced the pension committee to make its decision, and watched the pension plan's investment results improve. He found the new approach so compelling that he adopted the same investment strategy for his personal portfolio—again, years before most people had even heard of this stuff. His investment results improved, and he noticed another benefit: He was spending a lot less time worrying about his portfolio.

Rick realized he now had a way to put the markets to work for people and right the sort of wrongs he'd witnessed during his days as a young stockbroker.

Rick left Anheuser-Busch in 1997, at age 55, and went looking for an investment firm that shared his passion for an evidence-based approach, making the rounds of independent firms in the Midwest. Rick had built up a huge network of contacts—including successful executives from the beer business and at local banks, law firms, and other professional services firms—which made him a potential catch for advisory firms. But he told prospective employers that he wanted to use data and evidence to build his portfolios and to encourage clients to hold their investments for the long term. They weren't interested. Several people flat out told him that he was crazy: Neither he nor the brokerage firm would ever make any money that way.

They didn't understand Rick at all. Like Larry Swedroe, he'd already made his money. He wasn't looking for his next payday. He wanted to bring the benefits of evidence-based investing to as many people as possible. And so he kept searching until he found Buckingham.

He wanted to use data and evidence to build his portfolios and to encourage clients to hold their investments for the long term.

The folks at Buckingham employed an evidence-based approach, but their methods were more sophisticated than anything he'd seen at Anheuser-Busch. They didn't just follow a simple index strategy; they were using the data and evidence in a more refined way. Rick wasn't put off by the firm's shabby offices, and he didn't have a problem sharing a desk if he could learn new ways to boost his clients' odds of investment success.

As I listened to Rick's story, I practically vibrated with excitement. Our values and goals were totally aligned, and we had shared many similar experiences, but he was older, wiser, and calmer. I knew I could learn a lot from him.

Rick almost never ate lunch by himself after that first encounter. We basically created a lunch club, with Rick and I as charter members. We'd leave the office every day, take a walk down the block to get our blood moving, and then find a restaurant where we could grab a bite and talk about our work. Other advisors soon started joining us. Some days, five or six of us would wander down the streets of our neighborhood, looking for a table big enough to accommodate us during the lunch rush.

Eating wasn't really the point. Over half-eaten tuna sandwiches or plates of pasta, we'd talk about evidence-based investing, trading ideas about how to put it to work for our clients. We were like kids who had just discovered new friends, and who all liked playing with the same toys. We'd typically spend most of our time discussing a question of the day. It might concern anything from a problem an advisor was having with a particular client to the implications of some new data. Again and again, though, we found ourselves exploring some variation on a single theme: *Why isn't our investing approach more popular?*

Just as Larry faced resistance from the audiences at his presentations, Rick and the other advisors routinely met prospective clients who had a hard time accepting the evidence in front of them. Some people claimed to find the data unconvincing. But far more often, folks would say something like "Well, this sounds interesting. But I like my broker, Bob, and I really don't want to leave him."

It was clear that most people were rejecting us based on how they *felt* about their current situation, rather than what they *thought* about the data we presented. No matter how much sense our approach made or how many facts we could muster to prove it, we couldn't get these people over their emotional hurdles.

This was a big problem for the movement. Our philosophy was all about steering clear of investors' emotions, which so often got them into trouble in the context of the traditional Wall Street approach. We took a purely quantitative, academic approach to recruiting new clients. Basically, that meant we beat people over the head with data showing that traditional active management didn't work, fees were eating into their returns, and our evidence-based strategy offered better odds of success. When people had objections of any sort, we'd just throw more data at them until their eyes glazed over.

For people like Rick and me, the data was enough to convince us to change our ways. So we were especially frustrated to see that brokers *without* science on their side were still winning most of the clients and controlling most of the money in the market. We were all about substance over style, but style still trumped substance for a lot of clients. We hit this wall again and again. Each time we wondered anew: How could we stop investors from falling for Wall Street's marketing machine?

Over time, the other members of our lunch club moved on to other questions. But Rick and I couldn't let this issue go. We eventually decided that if we wanted

> *Traditional active management didn't work, fees were eating into their returns, and our evidence-based strategy offered better odds of success.*

people to abandon their flawed relationships, we needed to offer a better one to replace them.

What would such a relationship look like? After a while, some ideas emerged. What if we spent less time talking about data and more time asking potential clients questions about their hopes and fears? What if we stopped steering people away from their emotions when discussing investments, and dug deeper into those feelings so we could help clients manage them?

For the time being, we stuck to a just-the-facts approach when talking with clients. But our conversations about building stronger client relationships planted a seed. I began thinking about how I would run a financial advisory firm of my own.

The idea was a little presumptuous, considering I hadn't even worked with clients yet, but I didn't plan to go it alone. I imagined Rick as my partner. I saw us as complementary role players: I was young and ambitious, and I knew the science behind our investing approach cold. I had also learned a lot about the nuts and bolts of running a practice from my work on the advisor services side. Meanwhile, Rick had tons of experience working with clients. And he just radiated trustworthiness and patience—precisely the kind of person you want to see running a financial advisory firm.

It could have stayed just another crazy idea of mine, but one day at lunch, I floated a new hypothetical question by Rick: "If we were in charge of our own firm, what would we do differently?"

We began sketching an imaginary firm of our own. We'd offer

the same rock-solid, evidence-based investing approach, but we'd provide clients with more emotional support. Rather than pounding data into clients' heads until they capitulated, we'd teach them to love evidence-based investing as much as we did. That way, they'd be fully engaged in our growing movement, and they could help us spread the evidence-based investing revolution even further. When they did face times of anxiety and turmoil, we'd help them stick with their strategy and cope with the pressures that tend to derail investors and drive them to make costly mistakes.

We called this imaginary firm our "island of idealism." Gradually, we both came to realize we needed to make it real. We loved our work at Buckingham, but Rick had always been a salaried employee, and he wanted a chance to prove his mettle as an entrepreneur. I was young and, frankly, a little impatient. I didn't want to wait years to become one of Buckingham's key executives. I wanted to start making a big difference in people's lives right away.

Rick and I started meeting at a little bagel shop after hours and on the weekends to discuss running our own business. We spent a year sorting out everything from the profile of our ideal client to nitty-gritty details about how we'd handle reporting, billing, and trading. We decided to name our firm Hill Investment Group. It was the only time I've ever known Rick to ask for something just for himself. His whole life, he'd worked for someone else, and he told me it would mean a lot to him if we put his name on the firm.

In June of 2005—six years after I accosted Rick and asked him to join me for lunch—we announced we were leaving Buckingham. We broke the news first to the two people who had been responsible for hiring me in the first place—Mont and Bert. So there would be no hard feelings, we came prepared with a short memo describing our intentions and reasons for leaving.

Unlike the people at my first job, the folks at Buckingham were incredibly supportive. Rather than threatening to sue us, they threw us a going-away party. They saw that we wanted something we couldn't get at Buckingham, and they encouraged us to pursue our dream. Quite apart from that, our new firm would be a customer of Buckingham's advisor services business—so if we succeeded, it would be good for them, too.

Back in 2005, however, we were just two friends launching a business in even more marginal surroundings than Buckingham's cramped offices. Rick was building a new house, and we started working out of his partly finished basement while carpenters and painters tromped around above us. I scrambled to get all our licensing and registration completed, but our biggest concern was whether Rick's clients would follow us.

The first week after launching our own shop, we set up calls and meetings with the 30 clients that Rick had brought into Buckingham himself (we had promised our old bosses we wouldn't try to take any clients that had been assigned to Rick by the firm). To our huge relief, 28 of those clients agreed to stay with him and move their life savings to our new firm. We launched our business managing about $50 million for those 28 clients. We then spent the next several months trying to win new relationships with an approach that we thought struck the right balance between the head and the heart—offering the science of evidence-based investing combined with the emotional support of a trusted partner.

We really believed we could offer better service than anyone, but we soon realized we hadn't yet figured out quite how to do that. For all our talk about helping clients cope with their feelings about investing, we still weren't really reaching current and potential clients in the way that Rick and I had imagined. Many of our clients didn't fully trust our methods; they weren't completely committed to our evidence-based approach, and they still carried a lot of fear around investing. I was a little confused and a little discouraged.

Then something happened that turned my life upside down— and not in a fun way. It was terrifying. I wouldn't want to repeat the experience, but it taught me spectacularly valuable lessons. Among other things, it showed me, in the most visceral and convincing way possible, how to help our clients even when they were scared half to death.

Chapter 13

LOSING THE GENETIC LOTTERY

The basement of Rick's house wasn't the ideal place to run a financial advisory firm. It was very nice room, but you can't really invite a prospective client to discuss his or her life savings in the basement. Most of the time, we conducted meetings upstairs in the solarium, a glass-walled room overlooking Rick's yard. Meanwhile, I spent the fall of 2005 looking for commercial office space, and trying to adjust to my new roles.

I was now a business owner, which was thrilling but also a little scary. If we failed, Rick and his wife, Lynn, would be financially okay, but I'd be in trouble. I had married Lisa in 2001, and before Rick and I left Buckingham, I wanted to make sure she understood what we were really getting into. Driving home from dinner one night, I told her I was leaving a really good, secure job for a very uncertain future. It would probably be a bumpy ride, and she and I would have to make sacrifices along the way.

Rick was putting up $200,000 to get the business started, but we'd need additional cash to cover operating costs, including our own modest salaries while we waited for the firm to generate revenue.

I told Lisa we'd need to watch our personal expenses. There would be no fancy vacations, new cars, or expensive clothes for either of us. We'd definitely be staying in our 1,100-square-foot starter house. I told her it would probably take five years to know whether we'd made the right move, but if it worked out, it would be the second-best decision I'd ever made (after marrying her).

She gave me a serious look and said that none of those sacrifices mattered to her. In fact, she didn't need a warning from me about what we were facing. She already understood exactly what was at stake, because for a year, she'd been listening to me describe everything that Rick and I discussed as we planned the move. She had made up her mind long ago that it was the right thing to do. Lisa is what I call a heavy fact finder. She makes decisions deliberately and carefully, but once she does, she's confident in her choices. So hearing her say, "Yes, you should do this," was a major endorsement.

Rick and I were getting a lot of encouragement like that from friends and family. Everyone thought we were destined for success. Sometimes I wondered, *What makes them so confident?* I believed we had a good chance of taking all the lessons we'd learned at Buckingham and creating something special, but I didn't know whether we could attract the kind of clients we wanted—people who understood what we were doing and who wanted to be a part of it but who also had enough money to support our business.

Some of my anxiety reflected my conflicting emotions about leaving Buckingham. I felt grateful to those folks for giving me what should have been my dream job. They treated me incredibly well and clearly respected me, so I felt like I'd betrayed them in some way by leaving. I believed them when they told me that good things would happen for me at the firm if I was patient, but Rick and I had a dream that couldn't wait.

I was also worried about how I would adjust to working directly with clients. We had launched our business with the idea that we would engage people in some pretty intense conversations, encourage them to share their most important hopes and fears, and then respond to those feelings in authentic and helpful ways. And guess what: I wasn't really comfortable with that process. I hadn't had any training in that area, and dealing with people and their emotions wasn't as straightforward as conveying the data and evidence behind our investment philosophy.

My experience up to that point had been with advisors, for whom the topics of money and investing typically aren't as fraught. Now I was responsible for managing clients' anxiety whenever they felt like something was threatening their goals. Rick and I had done our best to prepare ourselves for these conversations, but I was struggling. I still worried about saying the wrong thing.

I also had another problem: I felt sick all the time. Throughout the summer, I was tired and achy, and I had a persistent cough. No amount of coffee could perk me up. When I tried to do something active, like playing tennis, I felt like I was moving in slow motion. Afterward, I'd need to take a nap. It got to the point that I couldn't even walk up the stairs from Rick's basement without getting winded.

At first, I thought the trouble might be allergies, but my doctor did a few tests and couldn't find anything along those lines. When I started feeling worse, I feared I might have something like pneumonia, but my doctor ran some tests on my lung capacity and still didn't find anything wrong. Around the same time, I had to take a physical and provide a blood sample for a new life insurance policy, but the insurance company's doctors didn't see anything weird in my tests either.

It made no sense. I could barely drag myself through the day. I was losing so much weight that my clothes didn't fit anymore. My eyes seemed to be sinking deeper into my head. By fall, my weight had dropped from 180 to 160 pounds. I put it down to stress.

By November, I had developed a new, even more disturbing symptom. Whenever I stood up quickly or walked into a dark room and turned on a light, I'd see rapid flashes of white light in my eyes, like sparks swirling in front of me. It reminded me of those old cartoons in which the characters see stars after getting knocked on the head. The flashes didn't disappear right away. At first, it took a few seconds to stop, but each day it seemed to take longer. Eventually, it happened whenever I moved my head quickly, like when I went to serve a tennis ball. I'd throw the ball up, tilt my head to follow its trajectory, and the sparks would start flying around in my eyes. I'd catch the ball, put it in my pocket, and stand there, clutching my tennis racquet, waiting for the flashing to stop. Sometimes, I'd have to go sit down, which baffled my partners. I often played with my dad and his friends, and they'd yell things at me like, "Come on! You're the young guy! Get back out here!" But I just couldn't do it.

By Christmas, I was very worried. I started timing exactly how long it took for my vision to return to normal after each episode. I hadn't told anyone what was happening, so I would sneak into a dark bathroom, flip on the light, then stand in front of the mirror until the flashing went away. Or I'd surreptitiously check the clock when I got out of bed in the morning and time how long it took for the sparks to fade. By January, it was taking five minutes for the flashing to stop, and I was *really* scared.

I had no way of managing this fear. I didn't feel comfortable talking to anyone about it—not even Lisa. She knew I wasn't feeling good, but I had downplayed the problem. I told her that I was just working too hard and that I believed everything would be fine once we got Hill Investment Group on solid footing. Besides, the doctors hadn't been able to find anything wrong with me.

Finally, I made an appointment with an eye doctor. I'd seen Dr. Susan Yang once before, a year earlier, for a routine eye exam. She'd come recommended by a friend, who insisted she was great. My friend was right. Dr. Yang had gone to Stanford. She was sharp and dedicated to the science behind her profession, yet she was one of the sweetest, warmest doctors I'd ever met. When I walked into her office for my second visit ever—this time under far-from-routine circumstances—she stepped back and looked me over. Then she said, "The person standing in front of me today is not the same guy I saw a year ago."

It scared me to hear that, but it told me something I really needed to know. I definitely looked as bad as I felt. Maybe this illness wasn't all in my head after all. I told her a little about what was going on and said that I had no idea whether this was an eye problem or not. I just needed to talk to *someone* who would step up and help me find an answer. The other doctors had just run a few tests and had given up when they couldn't find any obvious problems. I wanted someone who would keep digging until we had a reasonable explanation for my symptoms.

I just needed to talk to someone who would step up and help me find an answer.

Dr. Yang told me that she'd do her best to find out what was wrong. First, she said, she was going to look at the back of my eyes. She swung over a large instrument mounted on a swivel arm and asked me to put my chin on a small chin rest at the base. My eyes lined up with a lens a few inches from my face, and she focused a bright light directly into each pupil, one at a time. After looking at both eyes for a few seconds, she swung the machine out of the way and asked if she could feel my stomach. I couldn't imagine what this had to do with my eyes, but I gave her the go-ahead. She started pushing her fingers into my left side. It was a little tender there, but it didn't particularly hurt. After a few seconds, she got up, opened the door of the examining room, and called out to her assistant, "Cancel my appointments."

Oh, shit, I thought. *Something really big is happening here.*

She sat back down and told me in a calm voice, "Matt, you're either severely anemic or you have leukemia. And you're not leaving my office until we get going on finding out which it is."

It's difficult to describe what I felt at that moment. I was stunned. And scared, obviously. But I also felt relieved. One of the worst things about the previous few months had been the simple fact that I didn't know what was wrong with me or how to get better. Finally, someone had at least narrowed it down. What was more, she was taking ownership of the situation.

Dr. Yang told me she had seen tiny scratches all over the backs of my eyes, signs of bleeding. When she had pressed my side, she was feeling for signs of an enlarged spleen—and it felt huge. She wanted to do a few more tests in her office, but she said that I would probably have to go to a hospital to have special blood work done. In the meantime, she'd do whatever she could to get me ready to take the next step. Her demeanor was so focused and her directions so clear that I could tell she was going to do everything she could to help me.

I don't remember how much longer I was with Dr. Yang. It might have been 30 minutes, or it might have been a few hours, but the rest of that day is a blur. All I know is that Dr. Yang helped arrange for a new blood test that detected some form of leukemia. Two days later, I was at the Siteman Cancer Center at Barnes-Jewish Hospital in St. Louis to confirm the diagnosis.

I had to call my parents while driving to the hospital. *That* was a pretty teary conversation. The hardest part was realizing how upset my mother was. When the hospital finally confirmed the diagnosis, I called her back and put up a strong front. I told her how relieved I was to have finally found out what was wrong with me. I reassured her that I was in the care of one of the best cancer hospitals in the country and was ready for whatever treatments were necessary.

The trouble was that they weren't sure exactly which kind of leukemia I had. This meant I had to stay in the hospital for a few days while they conducted more tests. In the meantime, they had to prepare for a number of potential treatment options—including the possibility of a bone marrow transplant. They performed an incredibly painful procedure to take a bone marrow biopsy from me and said they needed to start testing family members to find potential donor matches.

They also needed to address my dangerously elevated white blood cell count. A healthy person's white blood cell count is between 4,000 and 10,000. When I showed up at Siteman, mine was over 300,000, and my blood was like sludge. It couldn't carry enough

oxygen, which was the reason I was feeling so run-down and seeing the weird flashes in my eyes. The doctors told me that without
treatment to get the white blood cell count down, I was headed for
worse problems—like organ failure or stroke.

The solution was a procedure called leukapheresis. The doctors
hooked me up to a machine that pumped the blood from my body
and spun it around in a centrifuge to skim off the white blood cells.
Then, they put that blood back into my system, along with a trans-
fusion of new blood. The doctors likened it to a very sophisticated
oil change. I immediately felt like a new person. For the first time
in a long time, I was actually hungry.

I didn't have much time to enjoy feeling rejuvenated, though.
They gave me my preliminary diagnosis soon after I was sent home.
I most likely had a rare form of cancer called *chronic myelogenous
leukemia* (CML). CML is the result of a genetic malfunction that
causes bone marrow to produce lots of diseased blood cells that clog
up the blood. Only about 4,000 people a year in the United States
were diagnosed with CML. Fortunately, a doctor at Siteman specialized in treating blood cancers like this one. They told me they
were running one more test to confirm the diagnosis, and they gave
me an appointment to see the specialist 14 days later.

Meanwhile, I tried to focus on Hill Investment Group. Rick was
worried. My first day back, he asked if I wanted to skip a meeting we
had planned with a client. I told him that work was the best thing
for me. I needed *something* to distract me from my illness. There

was plenty to keep me busy at work—including helping move us into the new office space I had found just before I got my diagnosis. Thanks to Rick and my work, the days were fine.

Nights were a different story. Like anyone with a serious illness, I began surfing the Web for information about my condition. Big mistake. For starters, since they weren't 100% sure I had CML, I began reading up on other kinds of leukemia, including some types that were pretty much always fatal. My mind went straight to the worst-case scenario: *What if it turns out I have one of those?*

Even if I did have CML, the information I found online about it was terrifying. Historically, most people with CML died within five years. And during that time, their quality of life wasn't good. They had to take a cocktail of medicines that made them feel like they had the flu all the time, and had to undergo repeated procedures to take bone marrow samples. I'd already done one, and it was the most painful thing I'd ever experienced.

I found one encouraging piece of news: There was a new drug called Gleevec, which controlled CML in 80% of patients and didn't have horrible side effects. But I found stories from CML patients who couldn't take Gleevec, or who had major side effects like vomiting and bone pain or for whom it simply didn't work. I couldn't help thinking, *What if that's me?* Then, I remembered that the hospital was testing my siblings as potential bone marrow donors, and I began to get paranoid. *I probably need a transplant, and they just haven't told me yet.* I did some more research and read that 50% of bone marrow transplant recipients died within the first year—and many others died in subsequent years.

The wheels in my head were spinning: Why was this happening to me? I was 33 years old and hoping to start a family with my wife. I'd launched a new business less than a year ago that was going to fulfill a lot of my dreams. And now . . . this. I had lost the genetic lottery. Maybe bad luck was the only kind of luck I had. If I had to have a bone marrow transplant, I'd probably be one of the 50% who died. If Gleevec cured 80% of CML patients, I could be one of the 20%.

In short, I was in a state of controlled panic. More than anything, I craved certainty. I wanted to know what was going to happen to me.

Chapter 14

DOCTOR'S ORDERS

I was still worked up by the time I arrived at the office of Dr. Michael Tomasson, one of Siteman's leukemia experts. I had written down a list of questions based on everything I'd read on the Internet, and I was prepared to hammer this doctor with all of them. If I indeed had CML, I wanted to know why this had happened to me. I'd read about a genetic malfunction called the *Philadelphia chromosome* that was associated with CML, and I wanted him to explain it in more detail. I wanted to know whether I was a candidate for Gleevec. I wanted to know what the next option would be if Gleevec didn't work. I wanted to know why a bone marrow transplant was being considered. My list went on and on.

A nurse walked me down the hall to the examining room, and I sat there alone, going over my questions for about five minutes. Then Dr. Tomasson entered. He was in his early 40s, tall, with light-brown hair. He was wearing a white coat. Something in his demeanor made me think of a college professor or an intellectual of some kind.

The first thing he said was, "Matt, we've confirmed that you have CML, and I know exactly what we should do."

He went on to describe Gleevec and how promising it was: 80% success rate, few side effects. The same stuff I'd read online. He said he wanted to start me on the drug right away.

This wasn't how I had imagined the conversation. I was expecting a lot more discussion about the science behind leukemia and the pros and cons of different treatment options. My mind was racing. I jumped in with my biggest question: Why had this happened to me?

Dr. Tomasson shrugged and said, "Matt, every human has a switch in their DNA that could cause this abnormality. Most people's switches don't get flipped. Yours did. We don't know what causes it, and I don't want to spend any of our time trying to figure that out. We need to get you healthy."

I wasn't sure what to think after this little speech. I had spent two weeks reading about genetic malfunctions and different treatment options. I was sure there was more I needed to know, but my expert didn't seem to care about those details. I held up my notepad and protested that I had a lot more questions to go over before we could make any decisions.

Dr. Tomasson looked me in the eye. "Let me see your questions," he said calmly.

He looked over my list, which was basically a catalog of my fears. Then he set aside the notepad and said, "Matt, I can answer those questions for you later, but I don't want you focusing on that stuff now. I want you to focus on just two things." He paused for a second. "I want you to get 400 milligrams of this medicine in your body. And then I want you to go live your life."

I had never heard anything quite like that from a doctor. It disarmed me for a second. Then, my anxiety kicked back in. I started asking questions about this so-called miracle drug he was prescribing: What side effects was I likely to experience? What about the long-term prognosis? What would happen to me in 10 or 20 years?

Dr. Tomasson's voice and demeanor didn't change a bit. He was totally cool. He told me that he would be happy to share all the clinical trial data about side effects—but we could do that later. As for the long-term prognosis, he admitted he didn't know. The drug had only been approved for six years, but in his experience, it offered the best chance for survival, with the best quality of life. Then, he repeated his orders: "Just take this medicine and concentrate on living your life."

He tilted his head down slightly and raised his eyebrows the tiniest bit, punctuating the sentence with a look that seemed to say, "Got it?"

And I did get it. I suddenly felt calmer. It was clear that he was sure about the path he had laid out. His confidence had a visceral effect on me. He wasn't trying to manipulate me, patronize me, or make me feel better by telling me what I wanted to hear. He didn't dismiss my questions as crazy or stupid, but he wasn't going to follow me into the weeds trying to answer them. He could see that what I was really fishing for was a sense of certainty—certainty that I'd survive this experience and that my treatments wouldn't be too terrible.

He was guiding me down a rational path, which led away from the anxiety.

Of course, no honest doctor could provide that kind of guarantee. Instead, Dr. Tomasson gave me the next best thing: an approach that offered the best odds for achieving the outcome we both wanted. His advice was grounded in his medical training and the latest results of a lot of very expensive, very rigorous, ongoing medical research. He was guiding me down a rational path, which led away from the anxiety that had nearly overwhelmed me since my diagnosis.

I don't often cede control of a critical situation to a person I barely know. But as I sat there listening to Dr. Tomasson, I realized that he was precisely the guide I needed in this situation. So I did exactly what he said: I went home and started taking the medicine and living my life.

I was already feeling better from the leukapheresis treatments, and working with Rick and our clients mostly distracted me from the fact that I had a potentially fatal condition. But over the next few weeks, whenever I felt anxious—which was many times a day, as I caught myself pondering my future—I reminded myself that the odds were on my side: I had an 80% chance of getting better. Even more important for my mental state, I reminded myself that there was absolutely nothing I could do about the other 20%. It wasn't like there were better options out there. Tolerating a few weeks of uncertainty while we waited to see whether Gleevec was working seemed a lot easier than staring down a bone marrow transplant.

A huge milestone came a few weeks later, when they gave me a blood test to see whether my blood count was normalizing. This is called a *hematologic response*, and it's the first step in determining whether my body was responding to the drug. It was an incredible relief to see that my white blood cell count was dropping. These tests continued every month for the next five years, with the doctors gradually using more sensitive measurements to ensure they didn't miss any signs that my body was producing diseased cells. It would be another two years before they could officially say my cancer was in remission, but I was on the right path.

As my health started to improve, I had more time and emotional space to reflect on my experience with Dr. Tomasson. Since our first meeting in his office, I had given a lot of thought to how he was guiding me through this process. He had the knowledge and experience to look into the research for me (so I didn't have to) and suggest the best course of action. He also made me feel like he was right alongside me, owning his responsibility for my care.

It struck me that there was a connection between how he served his patients and how Rick and I wanted to work with clients. Rick and I still did our best thinking over lunch. One day, shortly after I began taking Gleevec, I raised the subject with him.

I told Rick how anxious I had been before my first appointment. I told him about the way Dr. Tomasson had gently set aside my list of questions to focus on what we could usefully do right then. I told him how much better I'd felt after that first meeting.

He saw the contrast right away. We had always believed that when clients had questions, our responsibility was to answer them. In fact, we typically encouraged our clients to ask *more* questions, thinking that the more they dug into the science and data behind our investing strategy, the more confident they'd be that we offered the best way forward. But what if we were just helping people lose themselves in the weeds and adding to their stress?

As Rick and I talked, we realized what was behind all those client questions. It sounded like they were asking us to prove to them that evidence-based investing worked. So we obliged them. But they were often actually looking for certainty, some kind of guarantee that things would work out the way they hoped—which neither we, nor anyone else, could give them. When I asked Dr. Tomasson to help me predict the future (disguising my goal behind questions about cancer and his treatment choice), he refused to pretend to answer the unanswerable. He realized that I'd be better served by putting those questions aside and focusing on what I could do to improve my odds of success—or in this case, survival.

It was an incredibly important insight for Rick and me: Sometimes you can help people make better decisions by *not answering* their questions. At a certain point, they need to be told to set aside their need for certainty and focus on a strategy that, while it can't provide any guarantees, will give them the best odds of achieving their goals. Our clients needed leadership and direction, but we'd been letting them take the lead.

Then again, we couldn't help worrying about what would happen if we stopped answering our clients' questions. Would they think we weren't taking them seriously? Would they decide that we didn't know what we were talking about? Would they stop trusting us? It wasn't a risk we were quite ready to take.

> *Sometimes investors should set aside their need for certainty and focus on a strategy that, while it can't provide any guarantees, will give them the best odds of achieving their goals.*

We kept kicking the idea around: How could we apply my doctor's methods to our dealings with clients? As the weeks went by, I realized I trusted Dr. Tomasson more than ever. One day at lunch, I told Rick that my experience with cancer had felt like climbing a mountain. There was a monumental task in front of me, and reaching the end was going to be difficult. I could even die trying. But Dr. Tomasson, and Dr. Yang before him, fulfilled the role that I imagined guides play on mountain climbs. They'd made the trip before and had helped lots of people just like me get to the top. I still had to get my body up the peak, but they would be right by my side the whole way, making sure I stayed on course and had everything I needed to play my role.

I needed Dr. Tomasson to provide an effective course of treatment and help channel my energy and emotions in productive directions. He kept me focused on the long-term goal, instead of the pitfalls that might occur along the way. Dr. Yang's style was different from Dr. Tomasson's. She was more touchy-feely, but she was equally tough: From the moment she realized I needed medical help, she made it clear that she was my advocate and would fight to get me everything I needed to solve my health problems. In their different ways, both doctors gave me the support I needed.

Rick and I were beginning to believe that we might better serve our clients by providing the same gifts that Dr. Yang and Dr. Tomasson had offered me: Science backed by compassion, clarity, calm, and focus. We could promise to fight for every last advantage that would help clients achieve their goals. We would let them know that we understood their fears and could help them work through them. We'd encourage them to turn off the noise and focus on something that was genuinely useful. Like Dr. Tomasson—who had medical experience and clinical trial data on his side—we had just the thing: a strategy based on good science and hard evidence, which offered better odds of success.

My partner and I talked through these issues for months, but our conversations remained mostly hypothetical. The markets were doing well, and most of our clients were pretty comfortable with their investment performance. Our business was also growing at a reasonable rate, and we didn't feel the need for a radical shakeup in how we recruited new clients.

All that was about to change. The markets were brewing up a once-in-a-generation storm of global proportions. When it hit, that storm would transform our thought experiments into a blueprint for crisis management.

Chapter 15

THE HUMAN FACTOR

Our clients weren't the only ones feeling happy and complacent back in 2007. I was in a pretty good spot, too.

Thanks to Gleevec, which people were calling the *magic cancer bullet*, my health continued to improve. I had energy again, and the color had returned to my face. I was gaining back the weight I'd lost, so I was no longer swimming in my own clothes. I had felt so bad for so long that it was amazing to simply feel normal again. Having my health back would have been enough of a win for me, but then I got some more great news: Lisa and I found out we were expecting our first child, due in October.

Everyone's first child is a life-changing experience. It was an even bigger deal for us. We hadn't known whether my illness had affected my fertility. Dr. Tomasson didn't know whether Lisa and I should even try to conceive while I was taking Gleevec. Was there a risk for the potential child? So we called the scientist who had developed the drug, Dr. Brian Druker, at the University of Oregon. He said that it would be risky if I were a woman, but as a man, there was no danger. His exact words were, "Fire away!" Still, it really felt like a miracle when Lisa and I had a healthy, beautiful daughter that fall. We named her Harper.

Hill Investment Group was doing better than Rick and I had imagined. Our dream—which felt like a long shot—was to manage $100 million worth of client assets within the first three years. We ended up blowing past that goal: We had $120 million under management by the end of 2007, after only two years in business. Thanks to strong word-of-mouth from our clients, we were gaining a reputation as a great little boutique firm for investors who wanted an evidence-based investment approach.

It didn't hurt that the evidence-based movement was getting some good press, too. Financial journalists like Jason Zweig of *Money* and Jonathan Clements of *The Wall Street Journal* were writing articles about the efficient market hypothesis and evidence-based strategies. The idea that it was better to hold stakes in broad sections of the market than to try to choose among individual investments was picking up steam.

Just a few months earlier, I had been worried that the odds would never work out for me again. Now, I was basking in outrageously good fortune. I remember feeling incredibly optimistic about the future—like everything was finally heading in the right direction. But while my life was back on track, cracks were beginning to appear in the big financial picture. We typically tried to ignore the disaster of the day, but these cracks would eventually spread so far and grow so deep that they would threaten to bring down the global economy. It was like Ernest Hemingway's famous description of how someone goes bankrupt: It happened gradually, then suddenly.

The first real disaster was the collapse of the real estate bubble. Gambling on house prices had become a craze during the mid-2000s. A lot of people believed they could get rich by buying a house and then flipping it for a huge profit in a few years. Banks and mortgage companies fueled the frenzy by making bad loans to people who could pay them off only if their home values continued to rise. Wall Street then packaged those worthless mortgages into complex investment products called *collateralized debt obligations* that even their own executives often couldn't understand. Few financial professionals really knew what was in those investments or what the risks were. That didn't stop brokers from turning around and selling these time bombs to their clients, making huge profits for their firms. Mindless, shameless greed was the order of the day.

The dodgy mortgage companies were the first to fall. Their customers began defaulting on loans they should never have been given in the first place. For a while, the problem seemed isolated in the subprime area of the market, but soon the entire mortgage industry seized up. Banks simply stopped lending. Even people with good credit couldn't get loans, and with no one buying, house prices collapsed.

The problems then spread beyond the housing market. By 2008, even the biggest Wall Street firms were in trouble because of the bets they had made on those complicated mortgage-backed securities—investments that were now completely worthless. Seemingly rock-solid institutions like Bear Stearns, Lehman Brothers, and Merrill Lynch declared bankruptcy or were forced to sell out to larger institutions to save what was left of their businesses. By September of 2008, insurance giant AIG was on the brink of collapse because of its role in the debacle. AIG had sold a form of "insurance" on those mortgage-backed securities, called *credit default swaps*. The industry either ignored or was ignorant of the risks that credit default swaps carried—and now the insurer was scrambling to come up with cash to cover its obligations from selling so many of them. Since AIG was so big and was in some way connected to almost every other major financial firm, its problems threatened to take down the entire global banking system.

The more the wildfire consumed, the bigger and hotter it got. The Federal Reserve scrambled to throw buckets of bailout money on the flames, while investors ran for the exits. From its peak in October 2007, the S&P 500 fell 57% over the next 18 months—an unprecedented, previously unthinkable drop. The economy had shed more than a million jobs by the end of 2008. Newspaper headlines were calling the financial crisis the worst since the Great

Depression. Some financial experts worried that things would just keep spiraling downward. Regular investors watched their savings dwindle, and truly wondered whether they would ever recover from the losses.

I hope I never go through an experience like that again. But the crisis, which caused incredible suffering for so many people, contained a small silver lining for Hill Investment Group. It created the sense of urgency that had been missing from our client conversations, and gave us an opportunity to provide a new kind of leadership.

The first test came from our existing clients. Like a lot of investors, their portfolios suffered in the broad market sell-off. The situation didn't terrify them as much as it did other investors, though, because we had spent a lot of time telling them to ignore short-term market volatility and to focus on the improved odds of long-term investment success that come with our evidence-based philosophy.

We had actually trained them to *expect* a major market downturn every five years or so, showing them historical data on past market corrections. These declines, we warned them, would take a significant, temporary bite out of the value of their assets. But over time—almost always within three to five years—their portfolios' gains were likely to more than make up for such setbacks.

No matter what your philosophy, of course, you still feel like you've been punched in the gut when your investments lose 20% or 30% of their value in less than a year. We fielded our share of phone calls from worried clients during the darkest months of 2007 and 2008. But, thanks to my cancer experience, we were ready. Our investors were scared. I knew what it was like to feel powerless and out of control. I knew they needed a calm, confident voice to counteract the panicky, hysterical voices they encountered in the media and elsewhere.

Rick and I did a lot less talking and a lot less proving our case than we might have if this crisis had hit a few years earlier. When a nervous client called to ask whether we needed to change any aspects of their investment strategy to deal with the market turmoil, we'd flip the conversation around and start asking *them* questions.

We'd start by taking them back to the basics: "Do you remember what you told me your goals were back when we created the plan?"

They'd respond with something like, "Well, yes, I want to retire in 15 years and . . . " and so on.

Then we'd ask, "Do you remember the analysis we ran that showed how this particular mix of investments gives you the best odds of achieving that goal?"

"Yes . . . "

"Well, have your goals changed?"

"Umm, no . . . "

"So your goals haven't changed, and the long-term odds haven't changed. Why would we change your investment strategy now? Remember, if you're trying to time the market's ups and downs, you have to be right twice: You have to know when to get out and when to get back in. The evidence strongly suggests that no one—and that includes us—can get those calls right on a consistent basis."

Those conversations worked. Some clients just needed to hear our voices and feel our confidence. None of our clients—not a single one—panicked and pulled their money out of the market during those difficult months. Given the markets' ensuing rebound, we've never helped our clients more than we did those years. For all of our large clients, staying the course versus bailing on their investments has made a seven-figure difference in their net worth.

Meanwhile, the financial collapse was just the shock that many other people needed to question their old investing habits. Their portfolios were in tatters. The devastating results of Wall Street's speculative culture were on full display, and most investment advisors couldn't offer convincing alternatives—they were themselves part of that culture. Many investors were suddenly willing to try a new approach based on science and evidence. Some of those folks called us.

This was a huge opportunity and an equally big responsibility. Rick and I didn't want to sign up a bunch of panicky investors only to watch them run off to chase the next investment bubble in a few years. We wanted to be sure that every new client understood what we did, why we did it, and how that made us different. We wanted new investors who were truly ready to embrace evidence-based investing.

We now knew that getting deep into the weeds about the science behind our strategy wasn't the most effective way to engage clients. Instead, we needed to quickly and efficiently describe the core of our beliefs and convey our confidence in the path we recommended.

First, we'd share the essence of the efficient market hypothesis and its implications: There's almost no chance for any investor to consistently outsmart the market. Trying to find undervalued investments, we'd explain, is like trying to find a needle in a haystack. So instead of wasting our clients' time and money looking for those needles, we would buy entire haystacks. In this case, the haystacks were mutual funds that invested in collections of companies that together represented different pieces of global capitalism and should share in its long-term growth.

Next, we'd tell people that our approach called for investing some of their money in relatively risky assets—because risk offers opportunity. Most people don't want the values of their portfolios bouncing around a lot. But we'd explain that volatile investments tend to deliver better gains in the long run. Once again, the data tells the story. For example, small-company stock prices jump around a lot more than large-company stock prices, but small company stocks deliver significantly higher long-term returns. The evidence says that investors *must* accept a certain amount of risk in their investments if they want their portfolios to grow.

Occasionally, an investor might ask whether this meant they'd have to keep taking bigger and bigger risks with their savings in order to achieve higher returns. Not at all, we'd tell them, thanks to diversification. We'd explain that diversification works because different investments behave differently in response to particular market conditions. For instance, one type of stock might tend to gain ground when interest rates rise, while another might lose ground. By holding a mix of stock investments (along with some conservative fixed-income holdings), the day-to-day ups and downs of different types of investments in a well-diversified portfolio tend to offset each other, providing a much smoother ride to the investor on the way to higher long-run returns. Bottom line: The investor can have his cake (hold volatile investments with high long-term potential returns) and eat it too (cushion the volatility of his overall portfolio).

At about this point in the conversation, we'd try to make one thing clear: We were not offering any promises or even predictions about the returns our clients might achieve. The reason? No matter how much we study the evidence, we simply don't know how markets will perform in the future. However, we'd draw people's attention to the odds. We were confident that our investing strategy offered the best chance for success based on the evidence available. Until there was new evidence telling us otherwise, we believed it was best to act on what we knew, admit what we didn't, and be prepared to ride out whatever came along.

We'd linger on that last point, because we wanted new clients to understand that discipline is the key to success with an evidence-based investment strategy. We'd tell clients that the biggest

We were confident that our investing strategy offered the best chance for success based on the evidence available.

potential obstacle to achieving their financial goals isn't what the markets might do but what *investors* do—or don't do. Investors could destroy their financial future by selling all their stocks during downturns or abandoning a well-designed investment strategy to chase the latest "hot" investment. Alternatively, they could rely on the evidence about how markets perform and give the odds time to work in their favor. In the meantime, they'd be paying lower commissions, fees, and taxes each year, which could also make a huge difference over time.

We'd also contrast our style with the sales-driven Wall Street culture. Our message was that activity does not always add value. When things go badly, we'd explain, traditional brokers and advisors are quick to tell you to sell this and buy that. After all, they make their money no matter what happens to yours. By contrast, when the markets declined, we'd just look to rebalance our clients' portfolios. For example, if a sharp drop in stock prices drove a client's stake in equities from 50% to 45% of their overall portfolio, we might sell some fixed-income holdings and buy stocks to get the client's portfolio back in line with the original plan. Meanwhile, most people would be selling into the teeth of the decline.

This part of the conversation was meant to underscore our commitment to maintaining calm even in the face of chaos. Our office environment reflected that commitment. We didn't have screens tuned to CNBC, let alone squawk boxes. No one was on the phone pressuring investors to buy or sell anything. Clients rarely called to ask us what we were going to do about their investments, even on days when markets plummeted. They already knew the answer: Nothing.

So we thought we had a pretty compelling story: Our clients knew they were in risky assets for a reason, and that their overall risk was managed through diversification. They knew that they weren't going to pay excessive fees and trading costs. Most important, they understood that their evidence based portfolios offered them the best chance to meet their long-term goals. That meant they could ignore market fluctuations and get on with their lives.

This all came as a relief to clients who had previously suffered poor results trying to choose investments that would beat the market. At this point, many of them would have been happy to simply share in the overall gains of the global markets—which is really the point of investing—without taking undue risks. But by now, I had learned that we could offer the prospect of something a bit more appealing. It turned out that evidence-based investing also increased our chances of doing what most other investors were still desperately trying (and failing) to do: Beat the market.

Chapter 16

_____

STACKING THE ODDS

Returning from the brink of disaster can have a funny effect on you. In the space of a few years, I had fought a potentially fatal illness and run smack into the worst financial crisis since the Great Depression, all while trying to start a business. And yet, when those challenges receded around the start of 2010, I didn't feel battered or drained; I felt exhilarated.

Some of this excitement came from the fact that I now knew I had found my calling. Guiding clients through the emotional minefields of 2007 and 2008 had brought everything into focus. I finally had the sense of purpose that I'd been looking for since I had graduated from college and innocently plunged into the financial services business. I was equipped with an investment philosophy built on logic and science, and I understood what investors needed in order to manage their emotions. That one-two punch meant I could do what I had always hoped to do: Help people improve their lives.

Meanwhile, Hill Investment Group was thriving. We had gained $40 million in assets from new clients in 2008 alone, and by 2010, the firm was four times larger than it had been when we started it with 28 of Rick's old clients. That made us one of the fastest-growing firms in the network of 120 practices affiliated with the BAM Alliance. We had survived the startup phase.

> *I was equipped with an investment philosophy built on logic and science, and I understood what investors needed in order to manage their emotions.*

All this meant that Lisa and I could lift the austerity rules we'd adopted five years earlier, when I'd told her we'd need all of our free capital to support the business. The first thing we did was sell our starter house and move into a larger place that was less than a mile from my office.

One reason for the surge of interest in Hill Investment Group was the fact that we were delivering better returns than traditional brokerage firms. In fact, we were beating the market.

Luck doesn't explain those results—or the equally strong relative returns we've continued to post for our portfolios. The evidence-based investing movement continues to find ways to stack the odds in investors' favor.

To understand our success, let's use a gambling metaphor. Investing the old-fashioned way is like walking into a casino and placing your chips on red at the roulette wheel, or sitting down at the blackjack table expecting to get 21. You'll win sometimes. You might even win big on occasion. But in the end, slowly and painfully, the house wins. The odds are simply against the individual gambler. The free drinks, the cheering crowds at the craps table, the flashing lights of a slot machine paying out, the crisp-suited dealers and fabulous showgirls—they're all there to distract you from the math, which doesn't lie.

Market data doesn't lie either. So we've made a crucial decision. We're not going to try to win a few hands—we're going to own the casino. Our evidence-based, diversified investing strategy allows us to capture the growth of global capitalism, whether the ball lands on the red or the black. We make sure that we own the house, so to speak.

That decision alone is enough to help us beat most of the gamblers from the stock-picking and market-timing world. But here's the thing: Just as a good casino owner looks for ways to maximize the house's advantage, we also look for ways to increase our odds of delivering strong results.

The evidence-based investing movement continues to find ways to stack the odds in investors' favor.

In the casino industry, owners analyze all kinds of factors to determine the best mix of games to offer in their limited floor space. That's why visitors to Vegas are confronted with acres of slot machines, which are cheaper to operate than card games (slots don't require dealers) and which also encourage people to stay longer and bet more. Casino owners also look for ways to push games like roulette and keno, which offer some of the best odds for the house.

We do something similar with our investment portfolios. We tilt our holdings toward certain types of investments that have historically provided higher returns than others. How do we find them? Not through guesswork or instinct or so-called fundamental analysis. We rely on the evidence from some of the most respected institutions and brilliant researchers, which shows how different classes of investments tend to perform over decades.

Here are two examples. Back in 1981, a researcher named Rolf Banz[1] at the University of Chicago published the first study showing that the shares of smaller companies (known as *small-cap stocks*) have historically provided better returns than large-company stocks. About 10 years later, Gene Fama and Kenneth French[2] identified another important phenomenon within the stock market: the value effect. Value stocks, which trade at a significant discount to some measure of their worth, such as the value of the underlying firm's hard assets (real estate and the like), have beaten growth stocks, which trade at higher prices relative to such measures.

Evidence-based investors call these sources of higher returns *premiums*. There is still a lot of debate about exactly what causes these premiums and whether they'll continue indefinitely. But the premium offered by both categories—small company shares and value stocks—has been significant.

It makes sense. Smaller companies are often more sensitive to economic swings and might have a greater chance of going out of business. Likewise, value stocks are often found when companies have been beaten up a little—or a lot. Maybe they missed an earnings estimate or had problems with a product. Investors who are willing to buy those firms' shares in effect demand a discounted price. That way, if they hang in there long enough, they can reasonably expect some extra reward—what we call a *risk premium*. Without the prospect of such a premium, investors would just stick with the biggest, most established names in the stock market.

How much of a premium are we talking about? Between 1926 and 2014, small-cap stocks delivered a 12% annual return, compared to 10% for large-company stocks. Thanks to compounding, those two percentage points make a huge difference. Over those 80-plus years, $10,000 invested in small-cap stocks would have grown to $240 million, compared to $48 million for the same $10,000 investment in large company stocks.

Investors can reap the rewards of the small-cap and value premiums by including such shares in broadly diversified portfolios. That's why both small-cap and value stocks remain cornerstones of evidence-based investing. But they're not the end of the story. Like any science, the science of investing offers the potential for new discoveries that can improve our lives. The work of Fama and

French has inspired other researchers to dig deeper into the data and examine every corner of the markets, searching for other premiums that might allow investors to put the investment odds even more in their favor.

Most strikingly, researchers have found premiums that don't appear to depend on risk. For example, stocks that have done well in the recent past tend to outperform stocks that have done poorly. The resulting premium is known as the *momentum premium*.

This one makes some people in the evidence-based community a little nervous. They certainly don't want investors to believe they can just load up on a high-flying stock to boost their returns. As always, the idea is to identify a broad group of stocks with certain characteristics and then invest in the entire category (buy the casino). Moreover, the premium is defined by strict parameters, such as which performance period to consider and how long to hold the shares. Those rules, in turn, are based on research vetted by the academic community.

While the academics have been doing their part to discover premiums, the evidence-based movement has worked in parallel to develop simple ways for ordinary investors to take advantage of those opportunities. And like the science of investing itself, such products continue to evolve.

It started in the mid-1970s, when an old-school, mutual fund manager named John Bogle was contemplating the ramifications of the efficient market hypothesis. These days, Bogle, now in his 80s, is a legendary—even heroic—figure to many investors. Back then, he was the CEO of Vanguard, at the time a new mutual fund company with about $2 billion in assets.

Bogle figured that since mutual fund managers weren't good at picking winners, they shouldn't get paid to try. Instead, funds should just hold a representative sample of the entire stock market. That way, they'd avoid the risk of being in the wrong stocks. Better yet, funds could charge much lower management fees, saving their shareholders money and boosting their returns.

This idea had been tried a couple of years earlier with products available only to large institutional investors. Bogle created the first index fund available to individual investors, which today is called the Vanguard 500.[3] It was designed to mirror the performance of the S&P 500 stock market index, and now, it's the largest mutual fund in the world. The Vanguard Group has a big stable of index funds and has grown into the second-largest fund company, with more than $3 trillion under management.

Vanguard's funds compete with hundreds of other index funds, which together represent just about every category of financial asset, from large company US stocks to obscure corners of overseas bond markets. That menu of choices makes it easy for investors to build a diversified portfolio of index funds that will help them participate in the growth of the global economy.

Index funds remain a fantastic product. As Bogle predicted, they tend to generate higher returns than the typical actively managed fund, both before and after fees. Warren Buffett himself has said that he wants his assets invested in index funds after he dies. Despite these benefits, index funds also have drawbacks. A true index fund has to hold the same stocks as its underlying index, whether it's the S&P 500 or the Russell 2000. This means funds are forced to buy or sell stocks when the makeup of an index changes, regardless of price, tax consequences, or the characteristics of those stocks.

More importantly, plain-vanilla index funds typically don't fully capture the premiums available in different types of investments. Take small-cap stocks. It turns out that the smallest companies within the small-cap universe are responsible for driving most of the small-cap premium. These are *really* small companies—often called *microcap stocks*—which means that a typical small-cap index, like the Russell 2000, might not even hold many of them. If they do, their stakes in bigger small-cap stocks tend to dilute any microcap premium.

That's why some professional investors decided to build on the foundation of index funds by creating more targeted products. Companies like Dimensional Fund Advisors, AQR Capital Management, and Bridgeway Capital Management have developed funds designed to capture the premiums that traditional index funds can miss. For example, the more cutting-edge small-cap funds can concentrate on shares of the smaller companies that are responsible for the majority of the small-cap premium. Likewise, value funds can target one or more of several specific measures of value to capture more of the value premium than a standard value index.

These funds do *not* try to pick and choose individual stocks; we know that's a loser's game. But within a group such as small cap or value, these funds will buy every stock with characteristics associated with higher long-term returns—that is, stocks most likely to generate an investment premium.

Most of these funds are only sold through financial advisors. The fund companies don't want someone thinking they're getting, say, a typical small-cap index fund when they're really investing in a subset of that asset class. But these more precisely targeted funds allow advisors like me and my team and the rest of the evidence-based community to aim our clients' portfolios squarely at the premiums that we're trying to capture for them.

This is a very big deal. True, in any given year, the size of a particular premium might not blow you away. And sometimes the premiums seem to go into temporary hiding—as in 2014, when large-cap stocks outperformed small caps. But over time, the evidence tells us that these premiums show up often enough and provide enough excess return to make a real difference in investors' returns.

Our own results are a case in point: The diversified stock portfolio we use for our clients includes nearly 12,000 stocks and has a healthy exposure to value shares and small companies in the US and international markets. It delivered a 7.43% average annualized return during the 15 years through December 31, 2014—and that's after taking into account all the management fees our clients pay. By comparison, the benchmark of US and worldwide stocks that we use to measure our relative performance delivered a 4.58% annual return before fees. That three-percentage-point gap, repeated over 15 years, has huge implications for our clients' wealth. If you had given us $100,000 to invest for you at the start of the fifteen-year period, you'd have accumulated about $295,000—compared with just $195,000 if you'd invested in the benchmark.

Of course, we can't guarantee future results. We know that markets are unpredictable in the short run—and even in the long run. But we can promise that we'll keep following the evidence, wherever it leads us.

That's not to say we change our approach every time a new investment idea comes out of academia. We've set a pretty high bar to make sure that we don't chase some tantalizing new theory that doesn't pan out. Our investment decisions are rooted in a crystal clear understanding that the premium we're after truly exists—*and* can be captured cost effectively. Our mantra goes like this: A premium must be *persistent, pervasive,* and *liquid.* If it doesn't meet all three criteria, we ignore it.

Persistent means we need to see long-term evidence that it works. Ten or even 20 years of data aren't enough to convince us that a premium exists. Anything more than 30 or 40 years starts to get interesting, but if we can see evidence going back 80 years, that's reliable.

Pervasive means the premium has to exist across geographic regions or asset groups. It can't be an isolated phenomenon in the US markets or in some other corner of the world. We have to see the same pattern repeated for very long periods of time across the global markets.

Liquid means that we can actually capture the premium by trading basic instruments like stocks and bonds. We want to be able to gain exposure to these premiums through simple trades that make it easy (and cheap) to get in and out of positions when we create and rebalance portfolios.

I'm confident in our current strategy, because I know that all the premiums we target meet our three criteria. I also know that we can probably do better in the future. Researchers in the evidence-based investment community continue to explore new frontiers and learn more about the financial markets—making today an incredibly exciting time to be an investor.

Before Gene Fama came along with the efficient market hypothesis, investors looking for a more rational approach—something better than the usual gambling and guessing games—had little to go on. Fama and his followers offered a rational approach to investing, one that relies on data and evidence rather than speculation. It was a huge gift to the rest of us.

It takes time for new developments to win over the broader investment community. Vanguard's first index fund for individual investors was once ridiculed as "Bogle's Folly." But man, no one is laughing now.

Meanwhile, firms like ours are gaining ground as investors realize that disciplined, evidence-based investment portfolios can help them achieve goals that once seemed out of reach. They can spend less time managing and worrying about their portfolios and more time focusing on their families, their careers, their communities, and their hobbies—the "big rocks" that Larry has been talking about since the days when our investing movement was still so new.

Sometimes, I get so excited about all this that I worry I'm coming on too strong, that people might confuse my passion for a sales pitch. When that feeling arises, I remind myself that my colleagues and I are not pretending to have it all figured out. We just follow the evidence to where it leads us. When we do that, the best way to invest becomes obvious.

There's nothing to sell.

Notes

[1] Rolf W. Banz, "The Relationship Between Return and Market Value of Common Stocks," *Journal of Financial Economics* 9 (1981): 3–18.

[2] Eugene R. Fama and Kenneth R. French, "Multifactor Explanations of Asset Pricing Anomalies," *Journal of Finance* 51, no.1 (March 1996): 3–18.

[3] Actually, the concept of index fund management started in Chicago in the late 1960s to early 1970s. For more on the history, see: https://research.chicagobooth.edu/fama-miller/docs/the-origin-of-the-first-index-fund.pdf.

Chapter 17

WE'RE WINNING

The momentum I felt in 2010 didn't fade. If anything, it has accelerated over the years. The mainstream financial press is increasingly interested in the evidence-based investing movement, and their coverage isn't limited to a few columnists or buried in the back pages.

It's fitting that *Moneyball* author Michael Lewis was one of the first writers to examine the phenomenon, which he did in his 2007 profile of Dimensional Fund Advisors (DFA) for Condé Nast's now-defunct *Condé Nast Portfolio* magazine. *Barron's* jumped into the conversation with a January 2014 cover story on the evidence-based strategy behind DFA's mutual funds. *The Wall Street Journal* featured my mentor Larry Swedroe in a 2014 feature called "The Best Financial Advice I Ever Got (or Gave)." The piece put Larry in the company of old-school Wall Street insiders like discount brokerage founding father Charles Schwab and legendary corporate buy-out artist Carl Icahn.

The most telling sign that the evidence-based movement had come of age arrived in 2013, when Eugene Fama won the Nobel Prize for economics alongside Lars Peter Hansen and Robert J. Shiller. The trio was recognized collectively for their work analyzing financial asset prices, but the Nobel committee specifically cited Fama's work advancing the efficient market hypothesis and its impact in the world of practical investing.

It's sometimes hard to believe how far we've come. I think back to that day in 1999, when I sat on a crummy futon in my parents' rental house, reading Larry Swedroe's takedown of so-called active investing. Back then, Larry's book was sort of an underground manifesto. The people who read it were mostly data nerds who loved digging into the technical side of the financial world or investors who had been so burned by Wall Street that they were on a quest for something new. We were what the techies call *early adopters*.

Today, I can just pick up *Forbes* or *The Wall Street Journal* to read about all this stuff, or I can pull out my iPhone and instantly connect with a thriving online community of evidence-based investors. It's just much easier these days to plug into that conversation—which helps explain why more and more investors are voting with their dollars for a more rational, effective approach.

More and more investors are voting with their dollars for a more rational, effective approach.

Vanguard's index funds received more new money in 2014 than any other mutual fund family. The fund family with the second largest increase in new funds was Dimensional Fund Advisors, which is incredible, considering that DFA funds are only available through institutions and professional advisors, and that the firm spends no money on advertising. *The Wall Street Journal* summed it up best when it stated, "Investors gave stock pickers a resounding vote of no confidence in 2014."

We're at a tipping point. As more investors turn away from the gambling and guesswork of the old-fashioned investment model, they learn how powerful the evidence-based approach really is. We've redefined how you beat the market: through science. Investors who care more about outcomes than appearances or tradition will increasingly choose firms like ours over advisors who continue to champion the outdated model.

> *We've redefined how you beat the market: through science.*

We haven't won the war yet, but a lot of the battles are breaking our way. These victories would have been unthinkable to Larry and me in the 1990s, when we were driving around to gyms and hotel banquet rooms, trying to enlighten just one or two individual investors. Back then, we were total outsiders, nerds armed only with enthusiasm and a ton of good data, trying to topple a broken system.

Again, the *Moneyball* parallel is striking. Fifteen years ago, the

Oakland A's were pretty much alone in their attempts to build better baseball teams through data and evidence, as opposed to scouts' gut feelings and so-called common sense. By 2004, the long-suffering Boston Red Sox were using classic *Moneyball* principles to win their first World Series in nearly a century. Today, almost every team relies on data-driven decisions about players. A regular viewer of ESPN is used to hearing people cite statistics like on-base percentage or value over replacement player—the kind of stats that baseball scouts and managers once ridiculed.

Branch Rickey, the legendary manager of the Brooklyn Dodgers who signed Jackie Robinson, once said that baseball people were "allergic to new ideas" but added that events would force change upon them eventually. Many financial professionals don't like new ideas, either. But they can only delay progress; they can't stop it forever.

More and more smart advisors are breaking away and joining the evidence-based movement. We're also recruiting passionate young people just entering the financial services industry, who already know they want nothing to do with the old system. Hill Investment Group found one of these talented young advisors when we hired John Reagan in 2012.

John is a lot like I was when I was in my 20s: He was fascinated by the financial markets and really wanted to do something that would help people. Like me, he ended up in the training program of a large national brokerage firm and quickly realized it was far from what he expected. He was being trained to sell, and sell hard, for a firm whose overriding concern seemed to be making money for itself, not helping people achieve their dreams. One day, John looked around at some of the veteran brokers in the office. They seemed totally uninspired, worn out by the work they were doing.

John knew he didn't want to be one of those burnt-out salesmen in 10 years. So he walked away. He started talking to other financial firms, looking for a place that had a more client-centric approach. It was a lot like the quest that led Rick Hill to discover Buckingham, but in John's case, we ended up finding him through a bit of good luck. Hill Investment Group had made a charitable contribution to a nonprofit organization that runs a large outdoor theater here in St. Louis. John's father is the head of that organization, and he called to thank us for our support. As Mr. Reagan was chatting with a member of my team, he mentioned that his son was looking for work in the financial services world. The word made it back to me, and while I didn't make any promises, I agreed to talk with the kid.

I had no idea what John would think of our evidence-based approach, so I gave him some homework to do before he came into our office. I sent him some articles and a couple of books about evidence-based investing (including one of Larry's) and told him to let me know if he was still interested in talking after he'd finished reading them. For all I knew, he'd get turned off and decide to move on to another firm.

John asked if we had more things for him to read. Then he

stopped talking to every other advisory firm that he'd been considering and told us he only wanted to work with Hill Investment Group. I had a sudden insight into what Mont Levy must have been feeling when I was trying to talk my way into a job at Buckingham. *What was I going to do with this kid?* When John came into the office for a meeting, I asked him point-blank, "If I were to try this experiment and give you a shot with us, what would it cost me? How much would you want to get paid?"

John didn't hesitate. He told me he'd work for us for free for two years as long as he had the chance to learn what we knew and play a part in what he believed was an exciting, growing business. I thought that was a pretty bold statement, so I asked what made him so confident that this was the place for him. He said he could easily envision himself working here 10 years from now, practicing a craft that actually helped people. He was in this for the long haul. We hired him (with a salary).

We need that kind of passion to keep this revolution going. I haven't lost any of my fire, because I know just how much work there is left to do. I see it every time I meet with prospective clients. Many of these people are paying excessive fees for poor investment performance. Their portfolios aren't built to provide growth potential without exposing them to unnecessary risk. They are paying way too much in taxes. If they keep going the way they're going, they might not have enough money do all those things they dream about doing—things like spending their retirement traveling the world, making sure they can put their kids through college without crushing student-loan debt, or leaving a legacy for their families or favorite charities.

These are the people who are bearing the real cost of Wall Street's broken model. They're the people I want to help. That's why Hill Investment Group is still looking for ways to make it easier for investors to join the evidence-based investing community. In particular, we've continued to improve how we connect with our clients emotionally, so we can provide the kind of supportive relationship and leadership that they need to stay patient and disciplined.

One of our breakthroughs came back in 2009, when Mont Levy introduced me to a woman named Marilyn Wechter, a psychotherapist who devotes part of her practice to counseling people about their attitudes around money. Mont noted at the time that if there was ever an investment professional who would be comfortable taking advice from a psychiatrist, I was the guy. He was right: I was fascinated by her insight into the emotional factors behind common financial behaviors.

In one of our first conversations, I told her how Dr. Yang had made me feel held and supported during my health crisis. Marilyn confirmed my sense that we needed to create the same feeling for our clients. She also agreed that how people feel about money—what they want it to do for their families, what they're most scared about—is far more important to them than the numbers on a spreadsheet. As advisors, Rick and I need to be just as good at managing those feelings as we were at the technical side of investing.

I started bringing Marilyn into our office four times a year to speak to Hill Investment Group's employees. Her insight and guidance helped us take our approach to another level. She's taught us how to be better listeners and how to pick up emotional cues. Early on, she told us that we should start talking less and listening even more than we had been. She told us not to think of client meetings as the time to tell clients about what we do, but as a chance to learn more about them. We needed to ask them more questions and listen really carefully to what they said—and, in some cases, what they didn't say—to understand what's truly important to them. Then, we had to write down everything we heard or observed, so we could revisit those notes before each future meeting. By doing this, we would be prepared to continue the conversation and deepen our relationships with our clients.

It might sound simple, but it made an incredible difference in how we were connecting with clients. Before we met Marilyn, we didn't keep tissues around our office. Now, we have a box of tissues on the table for every meeting. We're not trying to *make* our clients cry, but we often end up touching on memories from childhood, key relationships in their lives, and their hopes for the future. One client wanted to pay off her sister's mortgage. When she realized she could do it, she began crying in our conference room. I asked her to tell me what she was feeling, and she said she wished their mother were alive, because she would have been so proud of how my client was taking care of her sister. That kind of thing happens a lot now, because we offer people both a rational investment approach that helps them achieve their financial goals and a relationship that provides a safe space to process their emotions around money.

Moments like that tell me that I'm in the right place, doing what I was meant to do. Beginning with my earliest childhood fantasies about being a grown-up, I imagined finding a way to make a meaningful impact on people's lives. After many false starts and difficult lessons, I'm doing that now.

I'm never going to say that our work is done—that we've figured this whole thing out and can't get any better at it. In fact, I know that the science will continue to evolve, and we can continue improving our people skills. But many nights, when I'm heading home from work and watching the sunset spread its orange glow over the red-brick houses and tree-lined streets of my neighborhood in St. Louis, I feel overwhelming gratitude for what's happened so far.

I'm thankful for everything I learned at that first job—all the scary, disillusioning lessons I picked up from men who were trapped in a terrible system. I'm grateful that my background gave me the sense to flee that world and look for something better. I'm astounded that I found it so quickly, and right in my backyard: a group of people trying to understand how the world really works and to do the right thing for investors. I'm amazed at those people's generosity toward me. I'm glad I was bold enough to accost Rick Hill on my first day at Buckingham and had the luck to encounter his wise and generous spirit just when he was ready to start a new adventure. I'm even thankful for my experience with cancer, which taught me what it's like to be truly frightened and made me value every day that I'm given. I'm grateful to the doctors who saved my life and who taught me much of what I know about how to help other people.

When I roll into my driveway, I sometimes take a moment to sit with my feelings about all this. We live in a complicated world. We don't know what will happen to any of us—even in the short run. Everything is uncertain. But we're not helpless. We can try to align ourselves with reality, which includes that uncertainty. We can try to understand how things actually work, and we can share that understanding with each other. My experience tells me that when we do those things, the odds of success—of happiness— shift in our favor.

I feel all this, the truth of it, in my bones. I remind myself to stay focused on what I *can* control and accepting of what I can't. Then, I get out of the car, cross the yard, and I go inside and get on with my life.

AFTERWORD

I hope that after reading this book you will see the investment world differently. Taking a careful look around you may help reinforce the core ideas that are essential to investment success: The financial markets are essentially efficient, so chasing winners in those markets is a form of gambling. And no one knows what the markets will do next, which means market timing doesn't work. The alternative is to invest in those segments of the markets that the evidence tells us provide the best chance for superior returns, and use diversification to manage your portfolio's risk. It's important to internalize those core ideas before moving forward. Evidence-based investing only works if you stick with it over the long term.

Once you're committed to the science behind the evidence-based approach, you can begin to do the work of changing the way you invest. It's possible to follow this path without an advisor, which will save you some money in fees. Most advisors charge somewhere around 1% of your assets annually, which can add up over the long run.

You'll face a few challenges if you go it alone. For starters, many of the mutual funds that my firm likes to use are available only through financial advisors or institutions. That means individuals working alone must build their portfolios using broader index funds or ETFs. Those tools are good—way better than actively managed funds—but they can't fully capture the investment premiums that more specialized funds can target.

As a solo evidence-based investor, you'll also need to develop your own asset allocation strategy with the proper mix of growth potential and diversification to deliver the returns you want at the level of risk you're comfortable taking. And you'll need to monitor and rebalance that portfolio over time to keep your assets within that target allocation—bearing in mind the tax implications of the buying and selling you must do to keep your portfolio in balance.

Most importantly, you'll need to be absolutely certain you can stay the course over the long haul and through the worst of the market's gyrations. My experience tells me that most investors need help managing their behavior at some point. For that reason alone, I believe that most people should team up with a financial advisor who can deliver a rigorous, evidence-based investing approach along with emotional support that will help clients stick with a long-term strategy.

That's not just my opinion. Research from the mutual fund

company Vanguard Group found that working with advisors can increase an investor's portfolio returns by three percentage points over time. Half of those gains come from behavioral coaching. The rest reflect the benefits of having an advisor manage the details of your investment plan—finding the most cost-effective investments to achieve your goals, dividing your assets appropriately among taxable and tax-advantaged accounts, and rebalancing your account periodically.

Like any major change, the transition to evidence-based investing can be challenging. But once you believe that an evidence-based approach is the best way forward, you can go after a kind of peace and satisfaction that most investors never achieve.

I recently met with a client who came along with Rick and me when we left Buckingham. He was a tough client, a former finance executive, and one of the most buttoned-up people you can imagine. This guy *always* wore a suit. He accepted the evidence behind our approach, but he felt like he had to manage every aspect of his investing life. He'd bring his own spreadsheets to our quarterly meetings so he could reconcile his numbers with our reports. He'd get worked up about even the smallest parts of the plan and always ask a ton of questions. But he was committed to the evidence, so he stuck with us.

Over time, he began to let go of the idea that he needed to be in complete control of his investments. He stopped obsessing over little details. It's been almost five years since he brought a spreadsheet into our office. He retired recently. Thanks in part to an investment strategy that put the odds in his favor, he and his wife have enough money to do what they want to do with the rest of their lives.

He showed up at our office recently wearing shorts and a Habitat for Humanity T-shirt. Rather than grilling me about his investments, he said he wanted to thank me. He told me he barely even looks at his account statements anymore. He's "completely rehabilitated" (his words) from his old habits of mind, which had him constantly thinking about his money and investments. He's focused instead on a list of 65 things he wants to do in his 65th year on Earth.

No wonder I love doing what I do. Again and again, I see how people's lives change when they break free from a broken investment paradigm. When you become an evidence-based investor, you can increase your odds of achieving your financial goals—and spend more time focusing on what's really important to you.

That's the real point of odds-on investing. It's not about beating the market for the sake of bragging rights or bank account balances. It's about increasing your odds of being happy and free. It's about living a life that's richer in every way.

So let's get to work.

ABOUT THE AUTHOR

Matt Hall is the Co-founder and President of the investment management firm Hill Investment Group. Matt dedicates his professional time to helping investors put the odds of long-term success in their favor by combining a long-term plan, evidence-based investment tools, and behavior management. In addition, Matt has led training for other top wealth managers, created new evidence-based mutual funds, and started an online group of like-minded advisors from around the world. *Odds On* is his first book.

Matt lives in St. Louis, Missouri, with his wife, Lisa, and their daughter, Harper.